PETROGLYPHS & PUEBLO MYTHS
of the
RIO GRANDE

PETROGLYPHS & PUEBLO MYTHS
of the
RIO GRANDE

by Carol Patterson-Rudolph

Avanyu Publishing Inc.

Carol Patterson-Rudolph   © 1990

AVANYU PUBLISHING INC.
PO Box 27134
Albuquerque, New Mexico 87125
(505) 243-8485
(505) 266-6128

Library of Congress Cataloging- in-Publication Data

Rudolph, Carol Patterson, 1950-
    Petroglyphs and Pueblo Myths of the Rio Grande / by Carol
Patterson Rudolph. -- 1st ed.
        p.   cm.
    Includes bibliographic references and index.
    ISBN 0-936755-13-X
    1. Pueblo Indians--Antiquities. 2. Pueblo Indians--Religion and
mythology.   3. Petroglyphs--New Mexico.   I. Title.
E99.P9R83   1990
978.9'601--dc20

First Edition

Printed in the United States of America

Dedicated to John, Amelia, Dan, and Natani

TABLE OF CONTENTS

TABLE OF FIGURES

TABLE OF COLOR PLATES

FOREWORD

It is a pleasure to write the foreword for this excellent and innovative work. I have spent my life deciphering, decoding, observing, classifying and describing various forms of nonverbal communication. My work not only includes my own culture, but also Japanese and several European cultures as well, that are basically different from our own. My specialty has been non-word communication, so it was a special occasion when Carol Patterson-Rudolph first took me to some of her sites and told me what she saw there.

I say this because, having been an old hand in the Southwest, I have always been both puzzled and frustrated by the images that I have seen on rocks in all parts of this country. Clearly they were not just plain doodles as supposed by some; in fact, the sun dagger at Chaco Canyon indicates that those images on the rocks were serious business.

It was also surmised that the Anasazi petroglyphs, unlike the Mayan and Egyptian hieroglyphics, were not a language-based writing system. If they had been, there would be telltale signs associated with all language-based systems, such as repeats of either lexemes or phonemes or both. The question was: "What kind of system are we dealing with?" Since all languages are important, even the nonverbal ones, they all can tell something concerning the people who use them. The closest analog is Erich Fromm's *Forgotten Language*, which is about dreams and dream symbolism which, incidentally, is (once you are familiar with how the system works) of a type quite similar in its organization to the symbolism in the petroglyphs of the myths in this volume. It isn't that the symbols mean the same thing, only that the relationship between a symbol and an event depicted in dreams parallels closely what one sees on the rocks in La Cienega. That is, the Uretsete and Naotsete myth when you actually see it as it is being interpreted, invokes an archetypic level of communication that could make this "rock language" accessible to a wider audience than the Tanoan and Keresan speakers who made their statements on the rocks so they could be read by others. This is *provided* that the investigator already knows, has used and is therefore familiar with dream language and how it works.

For people who live closer to nature than Europeans - with their high dependence on language - the dream, the myth and the petroglyph, thanks to Carol Patterson-Rudolph's insights, represent an unbroken chain that leads us not only to the archetypal levels, but opens up an entirely new world of insights and research possibilities into human consciousness.

Having said that, I should introduce a word of caution here. This particular communication system is not put together or organized in a way that is familiar to Europeans at those levels of awareness which they take most for granted. In descriptive linguistics, one learns early in the game to avoid projecting the investigator's own system and way of thinking onto the native language under study. That is one of the many reasons for using informants to tell us whether event A is the same or different than what we hypothesize as event B, or whether two sounds that are not identical, are allophones of the same phoneme or actually different phonemes. The only way we can know is to ask our native speaker if they are the same or different. We have been, until most recently, lacking this very component in the analysis and interpretation of petroglyphs. Is what appears to the uninitiated to be accidental or structural features of the surface (such as a crack in the rock), a structural part of the message or not? In this instance it is as though an imperfection in the paper or a ring left by a coffee cup were worked into our own communication system so as to have meaning.

Now for the first time, Patterson-Rudolph and Martineau, through use of Pueblo Indians familiar with the myths, have been able to work together with the Indians in such a way as to learn to actually decipher the message of the rocks. This is what this book is all about — no trivial matter!

We learn from the Tewa, for instance, that which we call petroglyphs, is in their language "rock writing." Patterson-Rudolph makes a strong case for "rock writing" as opposed to "rock art" and that to me is convincing. But if I were an archaeologist, it might not be, not because she hasn't made her case, but because by discipline and training the archaeologist has been oriented away from language-type events and toward artifacts and chronologies. In which case the primary interest would be in identifying and dating the "petroglyphs." However, I believe the future will be in favor of "rock writing" as the correct interpretation — a concept the archaeologists have for the most part rejected.

There is, in addition, as suggested earlier, not just the matter of dating and chronologies, but how one views the word. European cultures are centered on the word, and words involve linear thought processes in their use and interpretation. Rock writing is nonlinear, and while words are partially dependent on context for their meaning, rock writing is, I would say, almost totally dependent on context. The shift from the word world to the symbolic, metaphoric world of the Pueblo Indian is a great one.

Seen through the eyes of the Indian, the representation of a mountain lion is not a "picture" of a mountain lion but a reminder code that leads the viewer instead to the qualities of the mountain lion; the hunter, his strength, courage, stamina and the like. The entire process shifts from literal translation to metaphor and in this sense is much closer to the dream and the myth, which the petroglyph represents. As Patterson-Rudolph points out, metaphors are closer to *concepts* than words.

A Pueblo Indian colleague with whom I was discussing the La Cienega texts told me that the Tanoan petroglyphs are different from the Tewa petroglyphs. This suggests that hidden in the rock writing analysis there is the potential for discovering not only much more than is generally known about how the Pueblo Indians view their world, but because of these aforementioned stylistic differences it should be possible ultimately to identify the linguistic affiliation of different sets of panels and in the process record the movements of people not only in post-historic but even in prehistoric times. Should this prove to be the case, the rock writing expert instead of being a thorn in the archeologist's side, would become another ally— an ally because it would mean that it should eventually be possible to trace the movements of peoples within the Southwest during prehistoric times. This, in turn, would be deeply significant to the Pueblo people themselves.

From my perspective, Patterson-Rudolph's work represents a preface to a much larger series of studies to be conducted in the future — a first step in what should be an exciting and fruitful new field of anthropology.

Edward T. Hall, Ph.D.
May, 1990
Professor Emeritus
Northwestern University

PREFACE

In my travels through out the Southwest during my formative years, I developed a strong interest in American Indian pictography. When I entered college in 1969, that interest lead me to study fine art, attending the California College of Arts and Crafts, the Nova Scotia College of Art and Design and the University of the Americas in Mexico. I hoped to reach an understanding of the petroglyph images through art theory, but by my third year in college, I was not satisfied. I transferred to the University of New Mexico, changed my degree program from fine art to anthropology, and began all over again. Years later I graduated with a degree in cultural anthropology that had a strong foundation of symbolic anthropology. The thinking of Alfonso Ortiz and the works of Fred Eggan and Clifford Geertz influenced my studies at the university and are evident in the emphasis of this book that addresses Indian pictography as a symbolic language system.

In 1974, I made the acquaintance of a Hopi kachina carver who visited Santa Fe quite frequently. We spent many hours talking about Hopi petroglyphs, clan symbols and migration stories. He was interested in petroglyphs and their meaning and had recorded and photographed many petroglyph sites himself. He encouraged me in my studies for several years, checking on me from time to time to see how I was progressing. He gave me the book, *The Rocks Begin To Speak* by La Van Martineau, saying to me that Martineau had the only real understanding of the petroglyph symbols and was definitely on the right track. I followed my friend's advice and pursued Martineau's theories. I found that what he called "locator symbols" did indeed lead me to significant panels or trails or water, as Martineau said they would. I became aware that many of the more elaborate petroglyph panels were more often than not, pecked into cracked, lumpy and irregular rock surfaces, while the smooth rock faces nearby, were left alone. This characteristic of incorporating rock features into the symbol system became more evident as my studies progressed. In time, I was able to recognize basic symbols in many petroglyph panels, from a lexicon of a dozen or more symbols I was familiar with. I began corresponding with La

Van Martineau, asking for confirmation on some of my interpretation attempts with Rio Grande style panels. The resulting research and study of just a few panels and their possible interpretation took many years of research. I did not realize how complicated symbol interpretation would be — a far cry from a quick and simple method requiring only a basic lexicon of symbols with consistent definitions. My pursuit of petroglyph interpretation using Martineau's theories has required un-learning most of my "art theories." It has been a long road to interpretation by formalizing my studies in anthropology and stepping back from my own preconceived ideas of meanings, which are founded in Western logic and world views, and trying instead to understand the images from a Pueblo Indian perspective and cultural context.

Carol Patterson Rudolph

ACKNOWLEDGMENTS

I would like to acknowledge the continued patience and dedication that La Van Martineau has shown me over the years in teaching me so much of what I know about petroglyph interpretation. He has not given up, where other teachers would have, especially with the resistance I have shown in having to reorient my thinking so drastically. "White people may never get it," he has said in dismay. What I have learned, or think I know, barely scratches the surface of the material and cultural context necessary to interpretation of petroglyphs. To Indian people the theories presented here are readily understood. I have witnessed this phenomenon over and over again, when lecturing to a Indian audience.

My gratitude goes out to Teresa Van Etten for steering me to the specific myths portrayed in these panels. Her knowledge of Southwestern Indian myths helped greatly to expedite my research.

I would like to thank Greg Cajete, for encouraging me during the last few years and having the confidence in me and my studies to engage me in several of his curriculum programs at the Institute of American Indian Arts in Santa Fe. His intense belief in the importance of this body of knowledge has never faltered. I am especially grateful for his patient reading and rereading of the chapters from this work. His suggestions of resource material and scholars to contact have been a substantial contribution to this project.

Certain parts of the material in this book are based upon articles I have published in the *Journal of American Indian Culture and Research* in 1990 and in *Artifact*, 1988. I am grateful to the American Anthropological Association for permission to publish the "Uretsete and Naotsete Origin Myth" and to The American Folklore Society for permission to publish "Water Jar Boy" in their entireties.

My thanks to Edward T. Hall for his special interest in this study, and his ability to understand immediately what I am trying to convey. His remarkable perception and skill for integrating this information with linguistic analysis, semiotics, and nonverbal communication systems, including sign language, have brought to this project invaluable criticism, evaluation and inspiration.

I am grateful to Alfonso Ortiz, who has followed my research through the years and has been the greatest influence in my understanding of pueblo world views. I deeply appreciate the time and support he has given me in this field of study.

Rory Gauthier has contributed the major portion of Chapter 1 and I deeply appreciate his advice and information concerning the archaeological description of the subject area of La Cienega.

I wish to thank Larry Emerson, director of the NI HA' ALCHINI BA Educational Programs, Dine Nation, Shiprock, NM for his interest and encouraging letters of recommendation at critical times during the evaluation of this work by others.

My trips to the petroglyph panels with Joe Herrera of Cochiti Pueblo have been of special value and importance. Joe's knowledge of Keresan oral tradition and his experience with symbolic art, as a painter and artist himself, helped to substantiate the interpretations within the context of the myths and the physical setting of each panel.

Special thanks to Bill McGlone, a long time friend and skilled epigrapher, who has steered me towards a more scholarly documentation and presentation. His unselfish donation of time in going over this manuscript with me, word by word, to make sure that each sentence expressed exactly what I had in mind has been invaluable. I am very grateful to Nancy Olsen for her deep understanding as to the complexity of Indian pictography as a semiotic language system. Her knowledge of Anasazi and Rio Grande Pueblo petroglyph sites, Southwest archaeology and the current archaeological theories has greatly enhanced the accuracy of the data and footnotes in this book.

I would like to thank my brother, Mark Sink, for his fine photographs and his companionship on several of my petroglyph excursions across into the back country. The assistance of my publisher, J. Brent Ricks, and the people at OmniGraphics is thankfully appreciated.

I want to thank, most of all, my loving husband, John Rudolph, who has supported my efforts throughout this entire study.

INTRODUCTION

One cannot study the art [rock paintings] without studying the culture.
_____James Galarrwuy Yunupingu, (1988)

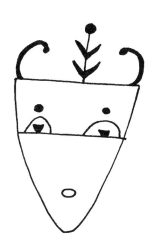

Martineau, in his first book (1973), based his theories of interpretation on the work of earlier ethnographers such as Garrick Mallery, H.R. Schoolcraft, C.F. Voegelin, and Edwin Denig who were concerned with Indian picture writing. Mallery in particular believed that Indian petroglyphs were analogous to a writing system based on Indian sign language. William Tomkins (1930) illustrated this concept to a small degree, in his handbook for Boy Scouts on American Indian Sign Language. Martineau followed Mallery and Tomkins' theories and added his own experience and skill in cryptology in his attempt to unravel the petroglyph code system and proposed decipherments for "basic symbols" and "symbol combinations" found in many Indian petroglyphs. He chose to illustrate his book with those petroglyphs that he could verify with historical documentation. He has learned American Indian sign language fluently and is able to converse with those tribal elders he encounters who know the sign language. Martineau travels throughout the United States, northern and eastern Canada and even to the remote tribes in Mexico studying cultural traditions and their relationship to picture writing. He has found some tribes still using the picture writing to a small extent in Mexico and South America and has found several elders in the United States and Canada who know the meaning of certain panels in their area, as taught them by their parents or grandparents. He has stated over and over the value of knowing sign language. That knowledge enables him to immediately recognize many graphic symbols in the picture writing and petroglyphs, because of the *metaphors* inherent in both pictography and sign language, that are based on "common knowledge."

The majority of literature today concerning "rock art" endeavors to categorize petroglyph images into groups, fragmenting an over-all panel of images and isolating each image from its context with other images. The labels given to each one come from an "etic" (outside) cultural view. What is different about this book is that it attempts to pursue an "emic" (inside) point of view concerning the meaning of the petroglyph images, and goes beyond the etic description of what the images in petroglyph panels appear to be to most observers.[1] This book treats each image as a symbol in an interconnected relationship that has meaning and purpose, within its own unique context, as derived from the indigenous cultural context or emic view.

I have applied Martineau's methods and symbol lexicon to the cultural area under discussion. My focus is on the metaphoric analysis that is culturally specific to Eastern Pueblo rather than pan-cultural comparisons. I hope to show how Martineau's theories are beneficial in clarifying the relationships between symbols and Pueblo myths associated with certain petroglyphs. Martineau stresses that ethnographic context and data are essential in any petroglyph interpretation. He states that the symbols of some of the more complex panels, when studied carefully, will lead to tribal affinity and identification. Mythical characters, ceremonial activities and religious iconography are elements unique to each tribe and distinguish one tribe's authorship from another. Clan symbols are often the same from tribe to tribe, but myths and ceremonies are culturally specific. Mythological characters and ceremonial items portrayed in the panels were the clues that led me to the investigation and final analysis of the petroglyphs presented here. They enabled me to identify the tribe associated with the myths portrayed in the panels. For example, of the Pueblo culture, the Eastern Pueblo are different than the Western in language, social organization and religious traditions. In the West, the Hopi are vastly different from the Zuni. Both have several clan names in common but do not share the same myths or ceremonies. Among the Eastern Pueblo tribes, the Tewa have a very different language from the Keres along with dissimilar migration stories, origin myths and ceremonies. These differences are important and must not be overlooked when attempting to interpret petroglyph images of one cultural area using ethnographic information from another.

The main concern of this book is the Rio Grande Pueblo petroglyphs and the myths of the Eastern Pueblos, associated with these petroglyphs. Each symbol is examined in the context of every other symbol engraved on the panel. Each myth petroglyph is supplemented with a graphic reproduction of the panel, or close-up area, to help the reader focus on the image under discussion

Eastern Pueblo oral traditions are the basis for the cultural context used to substantiate the symbol interpretation put forth. The meaning for each symbol presented is supported in ethnographic publications, thus narrowing the margin for misinterpretation. To the Pueblo, the images evoke memories of very powerful and important myths that lace together the fabric of their culture. Positioning, texture, proximity, repetition, abbreviation and rock incorporation are all factors of contextual significance. Each rock is also considered as part of the context, with every crack, curve, bump and crevice examined to determine if it may also be included within the context of the panel. There are instances where several panels are found grouped together and discussed in terms of their relationship to each other and story continuity. What is presented here, represents the present state of interpretation of the petroglyphs. As with all scholarship, some modifications should be expected as new evidence comes forth. Inquiries and opinions that could help broaden and deepen the understanding being developed about these panels are welcome.

ENDNOTES

1. The terms "emic" and "etic" are used by some anthropologists originated with a reference to linguistic studies using phonemic and phonetic analysis. The suffix refers to internal or external differences. In ethnographic analysis, the suffix refers to the observers perspective in regard to the subject matter.

1
HISTORY OF THE SITE

The petroglyphs discussed in this book are found on the cliff face of a small mesa above the abandoned pueblo village of La Cienega near the convergence of the lower Cienega River and the Santa Fe River at a place known today as Santa Fe Canyon, New Mexico. Many small streams, rising in the Sangre de Cristo Mountains to the east, join to form the Santa Fe River. The river flows generally west to the townsite of Santa Fe, then southwest along the Agua Fria Road for about 9 miles. There it turns south and enters the Santa Fe Canyon. This canyon, originally a fissure in the basaltic lava flow of La Bajada Mesa, has been further carved and eroded over time by the waters of the Santa Fe River. The river is joined about midway in the canyon by the Cienega River on the east bank. The two streams converge at the head of a small peninsular mesa that is the site of the petroglyphs. Figure 1 and Figure 2 are location and site maps of the area.

The geological history of La Bajada Mesa began with a series of volcanic eruptions in the Jemez Mountains, located to the northwest, that piled layer upon layer of basaltic flows and volcanic ash across the region. Subsequent faulting set a mass of material pushing upwards, lifting and breaking apart the layered deposits above. The resulting canyon is narrow and rocky, with basaltic rock formations very suitable to petroglyphic rendering.

Human occupation began in this area with so-called Paleo-Indian activity around 10,000 B.C. Archaeological evidence suggests a society based on a hunting-and-gathering subsistence. These people were big game hunters who used obsidian, chert, and basalt deposits found in the region to create tools and weapons, including the unique and beautifully made Clovis and Folsom points. Archaeological surveys along the Rio Grande within the study area indicate that Paleo-Indians camped and hunted there until about 6,000 BC.

In the succeeding Archaic period, from 5,500 B.C. to A.D. 100, the climate of New Mexico became warmer and drier than it is now. Larger game animals disappeared and hunter-gatherers shifted their subsistence base to small game animals and developed a

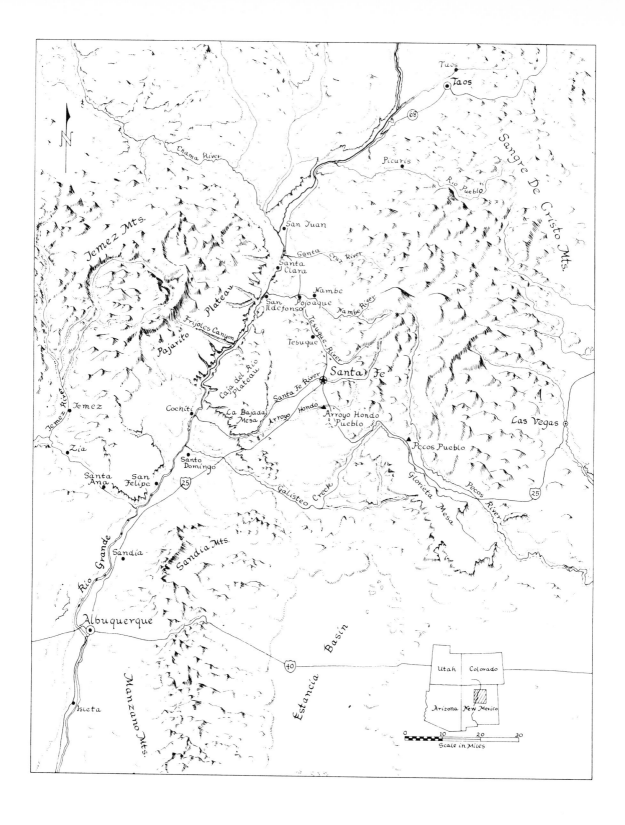

Figure 1.   Regional Map, showing the location of the study area in relation to the Rio Grande in the state of New Mexico

2

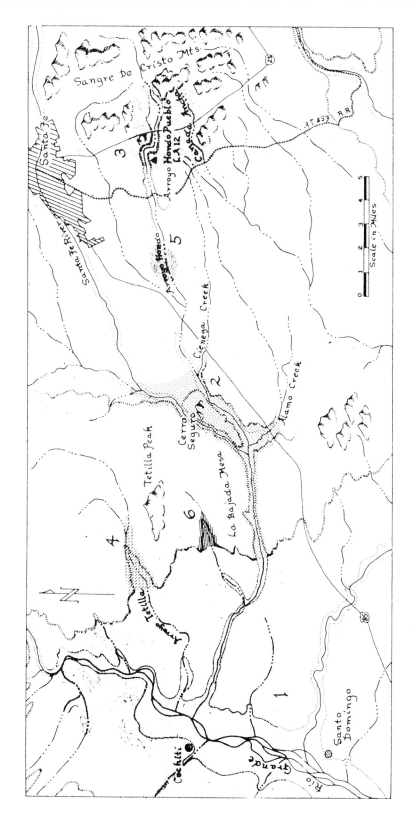

Figure 2. Site map, showing the study area located at the confluence of the Cienega and Santa Fe rivers, in the Rio Grande Valley, with the pueblo ruin site of LA 3, the ruin of La Cienega, and the cliff face along which the petroglyphs are located.

3

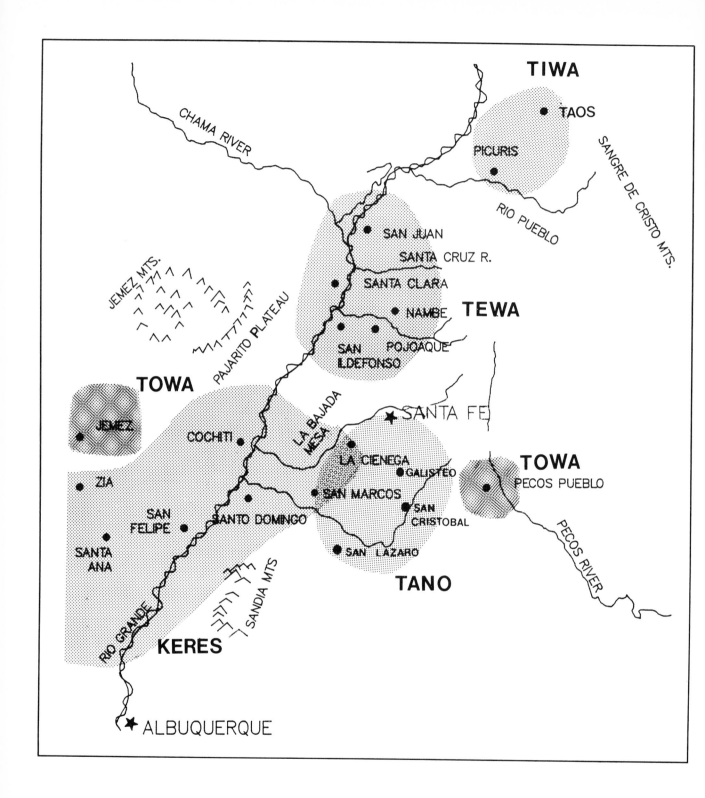

Figure 3. Linguistic map, the general areas of distribution of the Eastern Pueblo languages.

4

greater reliance on plant foods, at higher altitudes. These early hunter-gatherers traveled all over northern New Mexico and evidence of their presence on La Bajada Mesa has been found in various lithic sites. They gradually became the first permanent settlers and their agricultural activity and pottery types eventually distinguished them as the Anasazi or early Pueblo people at about A.D. 500 to 600.

The decline of the great Anasazi economic and religious society which had been centered in Chaco Canyon, occurred about A.D.1150. The years from A.D.1150 to 1200 marked a time when these people began to move out of the San Juan basin, north to the San Juan River basin, west to the Mogollon Rim and south to the Pajarito Plateau, to higher elevations in response to drought conditions, searching for areas where there was more rainfall. Settlements occurred during this time throughout all highland areas of New Mexico.

The 1300s marked the beginning of the era of "Rio Grande Big Kivas," and pueblo sites had open-air shrines oriented to the cardinal directions. By 1325 to 1350 the highland area civilizations shifted down to the water sources and the people built water control devices for their fields in an attempt to enrich their agricultural production. They built larger villages with big plazas and more numerous kivas which marked a distinct change from the previous period.

The descendants of the Anasazi immigrants from the Chaco/San Juan basin areas settled into the Rio Grande Valley and Pajarito Plateau. The Tanoan linguistic group that includes the Tiwa and Tewa Pueblo Indians, living between Santa Fe and Espanola, claim the northern Anasazi ruins of Mesa Verde, Salmon and Aztec as ancestral homes. These people eventually settled on the Pajarito Plateau north of Frijoles Canyon. The Tewa village of Santa Clara claims *Puye'* as its ancestral village. The villagers of San Ildefonso Pueblo claim that their forebearers lived in *Otowi, Tsankawi,* and *Tsirege*. By the late 1400s the Tewas had established large villages along the northern reaches of the Rio Grande. A linguistic map of the languages spoken in the pueblos of the region is shown in Figure 3.

A distinct Keres culture migrated from Chaco Canyon in a southern route to Zia, Acoma and Laguna. A southeasterly migration appears to have settled on the Pajarito Plateau, building the village of *Tyuonyi* in Frijoles Canyon and *Yapashe* and *San Miguel* to the south on the canyon rims. The Keres later moved on down along the Rio Grande settling at the sites of Cochiti, Santo Domingo and San Felipe.[1]

During this time, termed Pueblo IV or the Classic Period, immense areas were dry-farmed utilizing a technique referred to as grid gardens. It utilized lines of stones in grid formations that covered hundreds of acres of grassland. Planting was done along the stone lines. The stones served to hold moisture underneath, protecting a plant from the drying wind and sun and keeping the soil from eroding.

Gravel mulch was another technique used to conserve moisture and prolong the growing season. It consisted of small pea-sized to fist-sized rocks, that covered small plots of land. Each plot was bordered with larger rocks. Both methods also acted as solar heat collectors that enabled the ground temperature to increase and stabilize during extreme or unusual weather conditions. The mulch gardens may have helped to extend the growing season by a critical one or two weeks.

Stone garden grids appeared extensively along La Bajada Mesa directly across from La Cienega Mesa. Field houses with one or two rooms were located at the edges of large plots, and are believed to have been seasonally occupied by family members who tended the fields.

The Classic Period marks the beginning of open-air shrines called "Earth navels," which are large circular rock formations that open to the east. They are found located to the south or to the north of a village. The southerly placed shrines are usually within eyesight of a village's big kiva. They have religious significance for the welfare of cultivation and the planting seasons of the year. Earth navels that are located to the north and northwest of a village are usually at higher elevations in the foothills above the village. They are associated with game animals and the seasons of the hunts. The most important northerly earth navel shrine of the Keres today is that of the Stone Lions in Bandelier National Monument. Deer antlers are left encircling the Stone Lions as offerings for prosperity in the hunts. Pilgrimages to the shrine are made by hunters from the villages of Cochiti, San Felipe and Santo Domingo and as far away as Zuni, 200 miles to the south and west. The Stone Lions shrine is shown in Figure 4.

La Cienega Mesa is situated between the Santa Fe and the La Cienega rivers. It has a small ruin on top, designated LA 3, which was occupied around A.D. 1200-1400. LA 3 is a defensive location and commands views of La Bajada Mesa and Tetilla Peak to the north, the Jemez Mountains to the west, the Sangre de Cristo Mountains to the east and the Ortiz and the Sandia Mountains to the south, with access to water and springs within Santa Fe Canyon below.

To the south of this ruin is a circular rock formation identified as an Earth navel typical of the Classic Period and associated with the cultivation of crops. During the 1400-1600s most of the populations on the high mesas had moved into the valleys near the rivers. LA 3 was abandoned around 1350, and the new village now called La Cienega was established in the valley near the convergence of the Santa Fe and Cienega rivers, directly across from the mesa cliff face that contains the petroglyphs to be discussed.

During the 1550-90 period, the population of the Rio Grande Valley declined. Historians have postulated that foreign diseases, introduced by the first explorers into the area in 1541, took their toll by the time Oñate established a permanent settlement in 1598.[2]

The Rodriquez-Chamuscado expedition of 1581-1582 first documented the site of Cochiti, located on the west bank of the Rio Grande. From Cochiti, the Spanish marched up the Santa Fe River through the narrow Santa Fe canyon, which they called "La Boca." They encountered four Pueblos along the way. Among them they recorded the village of *Tze-nat-ay* that lies opposite the present town of La Bajada, and *Tzi-gu-ma*, near the confluence of the Cienega and Santa Fe rivers, where the *"Keres de las Cienega"* live. Historians today recognize La Cienega as a Keresan village.[3]

By 1610 the Spanish had established the City of Holy Faith, *La Villa de Santa Fe.* A few families settled along the Cienega River and built a small mission near La Cienega.

Figure 4.   Shrine of the Stone Lions in Bandelier National Monument.

The *Camino Real*, Royal Road of the Kings, was the main route of commerce, with a northern portion running through the Santa Fe Canyon, formerly La Boca Canyon, from Cochiti and Santo Domingo.

The little pueblo of La Cienega played an important role in the Indian uprising against Spanish colonial rule in 1680. Two Indian governors and captains of the pueblos of San Marcos and La Cienega, sympathetic to the Spanish cause, arrived in Santa Fe, August 9th, 1680. There they informed Governor Otermin that they had learned of a proposed rebellion for August 13 from two messengers who had been sent by the Tewa-speaking pueblo of Tesuque to incite their Tano brothers to participate in the uprising. Otermin reacted immediately and sent out word to the *alcaldes mayores* of each district throughout the province, warning them of the impending revolt, and advising them to take proper precautions.

Aware that their plans had been discovered, the Pueblo leaders of the revolt quickly stepped up their timetable for the uprising. Early the following day, August 10, the Indians of Taos and Picuris attacked. They moved south and were joined in force by the pueblos of Santa Clara and San Juan. By August 13, the Indians of Pecos, La Cienega, and San Marcos had joined the revolt. By the 14th, the Indians of Pecos, San Cristobal, San Lazaro, San Marcos, Galisteo, and La Cienega now numbered more than 500, and were one league from the villa of Santa Fe. On the morning of the 15th, the Indian forces appeared on the plains surrounding Santa Fe and gave the Spanish the choice to surrender or fight. The Spanish withdrew to the palace and a stand-off followed, until the 18th. The Indians cut the water supply into the compound and the Spanish concluded that their best hope for survival was to march south to Isleta. Being hungry and thirsty, their march was difficult, with hostile Indians watching them along the way. All along their journey, they found pueblos abandoned, churches desecrated and looted, and religious images burned. They were forced to travel all the way down to El Paso where they found refuge. The Indians of the northern Pueblos had their freedom for twelve years, until 1692, when Diego De Vargas reconquered the area in a return march north from Mexico.[4]

During the Pueblo Revolt of 1680, San Marcos and La Cienega were abandoned and their people joined the Tanos and others in the attack on Santa Fe and the Spanish. La Cienega was vacant in 1694 when Diego De Vargas returned, and efforts to resettle it in 1695 failed. In the following year, some Keresans from La Cienega, Santo Domingo and Cochiti were reported at Acoma; some of them probably joined the founding of Laguna in the late 1690s (Schroeder 1979: 247).

In 1695, the Spanish built a small fortress in the Cienega Valley, they called "El Paraje del Alamo." Travelers coming up the Camino Real could stop and rest overnight there before continuing on to Santa Fe, an easy day's ride of 15 miles.

For more than 200 years the Camino Real was the most important trade route from Mexico to Santa Fe, until the opening of the Santa Fe Trail from Kansas City in 1822. American settlers bringing increased quantities of trade goods, such as metal and cloth, found it quicker to transport them from Kansas City than from Mexico City. By the time the railroad was built in 1880, the Camino Real was almost totally forgotten.

In 1846 Stephen Watts Kearny took possession of New Mexico during the Mexican-American War. After the Treaty of Guadalupe Hidalgo in 1848 further changes in the cultural influence in this area were felt. The United States Army in 1882 built a road across the top of La Bajada Mesa to the west of Santa Fe Canyon and over the edge of the mesa with steep switchbacks down to the village of La Bajada. Santa Fe Canyon was bypassed, and in the 1930s a highway was built straight southwest from Santa Fe and down La Bajada Mesa on the east side of the canyon's entrance. With the building of modern highways, well to the east, the canyon is not visible to motorists coming and going across La Bajada escarpment from Cochiti to Santa Fe. Most visitors and residents alike are unaware such a canyon exists.

Since there are no public trails today, going through the canyon or along the mesa cliff face, the petroglyphs have remained well preserved. From their appearance in terms of gradations in patination, they span many centuries, dating from the Developmental Period around A.D. 900 through the Classic Period (Pueblo IV 1300-1540) to the Historic Period (Pueblo V, 1540-present). Petroglyph panels of the Historic Period contain familiar images such as Spanish caballeros, oxen, and Christian crucifixes. The names of the Spanish landowners also are carved on the boulders and span more than 300 years of family ownership.

The petroglyphs chosen for discussion in this book are categorized as Rio Grande Style, from the Classic and Historic periods in archaeological time (Schaafsma 1980). They are representative of Pueblo IV iconography, which have many similarities to images found in Kiva murals and pottery designs. Variations of these images are known to represent kachinas, clowns, Corn Mother, corn maidens, Spider Creator, the War Twins, Avanyu (the water serpent), and animal spirit helpers such as the mountain lion, coyote, bear, turkey, macaw, dove, crow, eagles, snake, and others. These petroglyph images are common elements that are also found in Pueblo oral traditions.

ENDNOTES

1. Jay Miller, in an unpublished manuscript on Keres culture, a symbolic study of Puebloan ethnology and archaeology, (1990) presents ethnoarchaeological evidence that defines the Keresan social structure in terms of "manly and womanly" attributes which are manifest in architectural forms such as round and square kivas, plastered either in mud (female) or lined with stone slabs (male) and are traceable in the archaeological record from the Chaco basin to the present day Keresan villages.

2. The dates and wording of the archaeological section have been paraphrased from a lecture given in 1986 by Rory Gauthier to the New Mexico Archaeological Society, Santa Fe, New Mexico. He has reviewed and corrected this part of the chapter. Gauthier (1984) lists the following dates for each period:

> Pueblo I   (700 to 900)
> Pueblo II   (850-900 to 1100)
> Pueblo III   (1100 to 1300)
> Pueblo IV   (1300 to 1540)
> Pueblo V   (1540 to present)

3. There has been much confusion about the tribal identity of La Cienega. Otermin refers to the people of the village of La Cienega as Tanos, as were the Indians at Pecos and San Marcos. Bandelier (1892:91-92), states that La Cienega is Tano and the name *Tziguma* is Tewa meaning lone cottonwood tree or "Alamo Solo" in Spanish, or *Cienega de Carabajal*, which appears in the documents of the Oñate conquest in 1598. Harrington (1907:469) can find no evidence that this name means lone cottonwood tree in either Tewa or Keresan, and Hackett (1970:xxxvii) concludes that La Cienega contained a mixed population of Tanos and Keres Indians. Schroeder, (1979:245-247) makes the definitive judgement that La Cienega and San Marcos were Keresan pueblos.

4. An excellent account of the Pueblo rebellion appears in *Artifact* volume 27, no.4, 1989 by Andrew Knaut entitled "The Pueblo Revolt of 1680: Eighty Years of Cultural Tension." Another major source is the *Autobiography of Otermin, Santa Fe, August 9, 1680, Revolt of the Pueblo Indians of New Mexico and Otermin's Attempted Reconquest*, ed. Charles W. Hackett, 2 vol. (Albuquerque: The University of New Mexico Press, 1942), 1:3

2
SYMBOLS, SIGNS AND METAPHORS

In symbolism, everything has some meaning, everything has a purpose which at times is obvious, at other times less so and everything leaves some trace or signature which is open to investigation and interpretation.
                                                                    ___Cirlot (1962: xliii)

American Indians have traditionally referred to their petroglyphs as "rock writings" or "writings" in the same sense they refer to any writing system. There is a firm belief that petroglyph images are intended to transmit information that is important, whether or not it can still be "read" or understood by contemporary people. Rather than consider the petroglyph images simply as abstract expressions that bear resemblance to real things, or, to label them as artistic expressions of the human imagination, it is important that a clear distinction be made between "art" and "symbolism" for the purpose in studying the Rio Grande Pueblo petroglyphs.

The term *picture writing* is used here to refer to any panel of images that conveys a comprehensible message. The term *pictography* refers to picture writing on rock as well as other surfaces and materials. The term *petroglyph* refers to an image that has been inscribed into a rock surface in some manner, and the term *pictograph* refers to painted images upon a rock or other surface. The term *rock art* is avoided because it has too often been indiscriminately applied in Western tradition to both symbolic and non-symbolic images. The term *pictography* is used here instead to refer to the symbolic communication system itself as it has been applied to rock surfaces. The term *art* carries connotations of individualistic conceptualism and refers to images that carry "non-common" knowledge to both Indian and non-Indian cultures. The concern here is with a semiotic study of petroglyph images to better understand how they express a "common knowledge."

Dr. Greg Cajete, a native of Santa Clara Pueblo has pointed out for example, that the word for "write" in the Tewa language, as it is used to say "I want to write a letter to my friend" is *TA AH' NIN'* . This same word is used for "paint" as in " I want to paint a picture for my friend." Both painting and writing are acts of communicating what is common knowledge (personal conversation, May, 1989). The term *art* does not accurately express this communication process without further contexting the specific way in which the term has been applied. The term *writing* more closely describes the use of a code system in regard to the symbols found in these petroglyphs.

Following the semiotic direction, art historians, anthropologists and semioticians agree generally that symbolism is an extremely complex topic. Anthropologists such as Munn (1976), the Tedlocks (1975), Levi-Strauss (1966,1976) and Ortiz (1975), address the emic issues of verbal and graphic symbol systems in their complete cultural contexts. Olsen (1985) examines the Hovenweep petroglyphs, in southwestern Colorado as an Anasazi visual communication system with the potential of a graphic symbol system. Visual signs are grouped by semioticians, into categories of use, icons, indexes, and symbols. It is beyond the scope of this book to present a complete description of the symbol system that may have been employed by the prehistoric Pueblo Indians and compare it with systems that were used in other cultures. Instead we will focus on the use of symbols as metaphors within the parameters of Pueblo mythology. A *symbol* has a defined meaning, which is based on a shared knowledge about that which it represents.[1] A *metaphor* is a symbol or related group of symbols that evoke an experience or concept of something, which in turn is used to describe a concept of something else.

Graphic symbol systems in general have a definite structure and syntax. Cirlot (Dictionary of Symbols,1962:liii-liv), believes Western European symbol syntax may function in four different ways:

1. The successive manner, in which one symbol is placed alongside another; their meanings do not combine and are not even interrelated.
2. The progressive manner, in which the meanings of the symbols do not interact but represent different stages in the symbolic process.
3. The composite manner, in which the proximity of the symbols brings about change and creates complex meanings; here a synthesis is involved and not merely a mixture of their meanings.
4. The dramatic manner, in which there is an interaction between the groups and all the potentialities of the proceeding groups are synthesized.

Indian symbol systems, however, may be structured differently in some ways: 1) they do not read successively, in a linear manner, as is so characteristic of graphic symbol systems of cultures who use alphabetic writing systems; and 2) they differ from the progressive manner in that they *do* interact with one another and their meaning is dependent upon this interaction.

Indian pictography is composed of graphic symbols with basic meanings and many extensions; like any language, in different contexts, different extensions apply. Symbols may change meaning when the context changes. These are called symbol extensions. This is the reason that studies of symbol lexicons cannot be complete if the lexical symbols are studied exclusive of the context in which they are found.

In the English language, the majority of words (sound symbols), listed in any dictionary are accompanied by more than one definition. The word "solution" can be used in completely dissimilar contexts. For the word "hard," the dictionary lists a full page of semantic extensions to its meaning in different contexts. Semantic extensions are a common trait in most languages. The Western Apaches, for example, apply the same words for human body parts that they do for corresponding parts of an automobile. Thus, if a person were speaking in Apache of his liver malfunctioning, the context of the entire conversation would determine whether the person needed hospitalization or the battery changed in his car. [2]

Indian pictography is a language or symbol system. The symbols have meaning and semantic extensions that convey additional meanings. For example, the terrace symbol in the Southwest generally means "piled up." The Kiowas have used this symbol to represent rocks "piled up" in describing their defense against an attack by the Mexicans at Hueco Tanks, as explained by Martineau, (1973:82). The Navajos used it to describe the stockpiles of food that were destroyed by the U.S. soldiers in their attempt to starve and conquer them. Figure 5 gives an example from the Navajo Panel in Largo Canyon that illustrates the 1865 Kit Carson Campaign depicting the corn that was piled and burned by the soldiers, (Martineau 1973:101).

Figure 6 shows the Iariko Panel, with a *Sipapu* or dwelling place shown as a terraced

Figure 5.   Navajo record of Kit Carson's Navajo Campaign of 1863-64 found in Largo Canyon, New Mexico. The terrace symbol is used to describe the "piled up" corn the soldiers piled and burned. (After Martineau 1973)

symbol as discussed in Chapter 6. The "piled up" symbol has other extended meanings when used with other symbols to represent sacred altars or piled up cumulus clouds. Figure 7, from the Kuaua ruins, depicts a terraced altar, symbolizing winter snow; rainbow, signifying the pollen path (Dutton; 1963:89 plate J-34). Dutton (1963) interprets this symbol as an altar and in some cases cloud altars.

The "Cloud-Blower" petroglyph panel in Figure 8, is interpreted as depicting a "cloud blower" because it uses the terrace symbol turned horizontally and two cloud symbols are joined with a connecting line. Dumarest (1919:182) writes that when the clouds come, the women are wearing the terraced design they call *haetchoni*, (steps) behind the clouds. When the clouds come, people will say, "Here comes the *haetchoni*." In this panel, the altar/cloud symbols are used in context with a fertility figure holding a cloud-blower (not a flute). Examples of cloud-blowers are found in prehistoric sites throughout the Southwest and are distinguished by their enlarged or flanged ends. The cloud blower should not be confused with a flute, which has a tapered end. Figure 9 illustrates a ceremonial cloud blower from a Pueblo IV site within the study area. The cloud blower as a symbol conveys the relationship between smoke and rain. It is believed that smoke makes the mist and feeds the clouds so they grow larger and join together (Parsons 1939:370-372). Note the figure does not have a hunch back, but rather a pack or burden basket that he carries lower down on his back, below his shoulders. Figures similar to this are often collectively called "Kokopelli" and clarification of this figure is discussed in Chapter 3.

Figure 6.   Section of the Iariko panel showing the "terrace" symbol. This petroglyph is found on the cliff face at La Cienega.

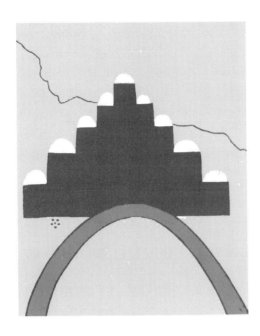

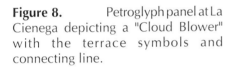

Figure 7. The kiva murals at Kuaua ruin showing the "terrace symbol. (After Dutton, 1963 Fig. 78, pg. 89.)

Figure 8. Petroglyph panel at La Cienega depicting a "Cloud Blower" with the terrace symbols and connecting line.

Figure 9. Ceremonial cloud blower. (School of American Research Collection)

15

METAPHOR

Metaphor is present in every part of our life: in literature, in art, in the media, even in our daily conversations. It saturates our language in ways of which we are hardly aware. Most of all, metaphor is part of our conceptualizing process. We think in terms of metaphors in order to convey concepts difficult to express in plain language. Metaphoric analogies allow a meaning to be conveyed within a more familiar structure. Metaphor is used to describe something in terms of something else; "a figure of speech in which a word, term or phrase is applied to something to which it is not literally applicable, in order to suggest a resemblance: *She is the flower of my life.*" (New Webster Dictionary of the English Language). The structure found within a common experience is used to describe the structure of something unfamiliar. Metaphor is used to enhance the meaning of an experience, making that which is mundane, extraordinary.

Metaphor, too, has structure. It contains participants such as people, animals, or plants. It has parts that consist of activities, conversations, or adventures. It has stages that consist of conditions that change as one passes through each stage like an initiation process. It has a linear sequence, where the participants in their actions portray meaning that is culturally defined by the order and positioning of each participant. There is cause and effect and a purpose of teaching a truth that would otherwise be obscure.

The most important point to understand when talking about metaphor is that it enables us to make a link between our experience and a new concept. The language of metaphor creates a parallel structure between the known and the unknown. Metaphor allows a culture to define its parameters with social behavior, ritual, and cosmology.

In Western culture the most predominant and consistent theme since Classical Greece has been the interrelationship between Man and Nature. By objectifying Nature and studying its properties, Western Man has come to believe he has to dominate and control Nature. He strives to observe the world around him "objectively" as a separate entity in order to learn the "truth" about his world. He separates everything in order to look at it apart from other things and to gain an understanding of its reality. He classifies everything around him into categories that include physical, intellectual, spiritual and emotional realms that are separate from himself.

The Christian/Judaic metaphors contain an after-world in the sky for those who live a virtuous life. Those persons who are considered evil may, of course, face an afterlife below the ground. Metaphors are created consistent with this theme throughout the literature in Christian/Judaic culture. They extend to the concepts that the direction up is good, and down is bad; rational is better than emotional judgment; more is better than less; and so on. Like our physical bodies, which stand erect, the head ranks the highest and the metaphor of the brain is of greater value than that of the heart, which is better than our stomach, which is better than our groin and so on down to our feet that trod upon the earth. The earth is dirty and unclean, whereas the fluffy white clouds of the heavens are divine. The Western culture rates itself above all other life forms, putting plants at the lower end, and human life at the top. The Western world has picked north as the top of the Earth, and we orient our perception of the globe in terms of top and bottom, above and below, Australia being "down under."

The pueblo cultures, on the other hand, orient more to the south in the direction of the sun. To the pueblo, the Earth is their Mother and they belong more to the Earth than the Earth does to them. Their very existence is like that of the plants they cultivate (Ortiz 1989). Time is not conceived in a linear fashion, but more of a continuum marked by significant events, rituals, and personal growth. Pueblo metaphors reflect their strong alliance with the Earth, and equality with all life forms in a manner that is quite different from the Western hierarchical perception.

Metaphors that people use in their everyday language tell a lot about how they perceive the world. A clash of cultural metaphors did indeed occur when the Spanish Inquisition and Catholicism were imposed upon the pueblos and their kachina societies. It occurred across many levels of communication, which itself depended upon finding a metaphor that would convey a common experience. The clash of religious concepts is reflected in this passage from the early Spanish chronicles:

> Another of the duties of an *alcalde mayor* was to announce in all the settlements and pueblos of his district,...the decrees of the governor in Santa Fe. When, to the horror of the friars, Lopez de Medizabal decreed that the Indians should resume their ceremonial dances, Gonzalez Bernal did his duty. According to the missionary at Galisteo, "the Tanos of that pueblo, San Cristobal, San Lazaro, and La Cienega were only too happy to oblige with some evil and idolatrous dances called kachinas, from which idolatry followed in these pueblos."
>
> Kessell 1979:178

Governor Juan Ignacio Flores Mogollon of Santa Fe, January 20,1714 is reported to have said,

> In as much as I have had word that at the pueblo of Pecos a partially subterranean room in the form of a kiva or *coi* [a kiva within a house block] has been built apart from the pueblo under the pretext of the women getting together to spin; in as much as its door should open on the street, and the king our lord (God save him) has ordered all his ministers to observe with utmost diligence that such rooms are not built in the pueblos because of the great superstitious and idolatrous abuses that are committed, as is of record; and in as much as there are in addition to this one others in said pueblo, I order the *alcalde mayor* of that district to go immediately and ascertain if it is true. If it is, he will make them destroy and demolish it immediately.
>
> Kessell 1979:299

Pueblo religious concepts differed from those of the Spanish and the Americans who followed. The Christian/Judaic concept proposes a separation between man and nature resulting in his exploitation and domination of the land. The pueblo, in particular, strives to keep man in balance with nature and integrate his actions in a way that is productive to both. Strict taboos and formal rituals are instituted to insure the balance of nature as it relates to man, lest droughts and disease should be the consequence. To the pueblo, everything is alive with spirit, including rocks, mountains and lakes.

The contrast in belief systems between Spanish and Indian cultures was encountered on many tragic occasions. Differences are found in the metaphors of both cultures. This contrast in metaphors is important to understand if a person from one culture is trying to interpret the visual images of another culture's metaphors. The metaphors of the pueblos are grounded in real-life experiences that are found in nature. This is reflected in the pueblo passage :

> Now this is what we believe. The mother of us all is the Earth. The Father is the sun. The Grandfather is the Creator who bathed us with his mind, and gave life to all things. The Brother is the beasts and trees. The Sister is that with wings. We are the Children of the Earth and do it no harm in any way. Nor do we offend the sun by not greeting it at dawn. We praise our Grandfather for his creation. We share the same breath together - the beast, the trees, the birds, the man.
>
> Wood 1974:18

The metaphors chosen by Indians are largely drawn from nature, the weather, the natural surroundings, and plant and animal life. This excerpt from Chief Seattle's letter to the people of Washington in 1854 is an example of Indian oration and produces insight into their cultural context:

> Day and night cannot dwell together. The Red Man has ever fled the approach of the white man, as the changing mist on the mountain side flees before the blazing sun. ....No bright star hovers above his horizon. Sad-voiced winds moan in the distance. Some Gate of our race is on the Red Man's trail, and where ever he goes he will still hear the sure approaching footsteps of his fell destroyer and prepare to solidly meet his doom, as does the wounded doe that hears the approaching footsteps of the hunter ...The white man will never be alone. Let him be just and deal kindly with my people, for the dead are not powerless. Dead - did I say? There is no death. Only a change in worlds!

The focus of this book is on the metaphors used by the pueblos, particularly the Rio Grande pueblos, and how these metaphors are applied as visual images in their petroglyphs. It is impossible to interpret the symbols found in the petroglyphs without knowing the metaphors that were employed by the culture. For example, the metaphor of a corn plant is used by all the pueblos in reference to life and the various stages of growth from birth, through childhood, adulthood, and old age. They consider themselves the Children of the Earth. According to Alfonso Ortiz, the pueblos left monuments attesting to their belief that they grew up out of the ground, out of the earth like the corn plant, their mother. Hovenweep, he believes, is a giant emergence place. The towers in the canyon were thought to be used for fortification by early archaeologists, but now they think they may have had more of an economic or religious function. Ortiz (1989) believes they were metaphoric manifestations of the emergence stories. They are attempts to replicate on the surface of the ground the process of emergence from a prior life within the Earth of three previous worlds to the fourth, present world.

The Road of Life metaphor is also dominant in pueblo expression. The "roads of Chaco Canyon" are a puzzle because they too, like the towers, do not serve a purpose conducive to Western logic. Many roads "go nowhere," or are found in twos or fours, running parallel for a distance before stopping. Archaeologists are discovering that the roads make more sense if interpreted through the ethnographic records and the pueblo metaphors are considered.[3] Several of the Chaco roads lead to prominent natural formations that may have been shrines which are an important aspect of pueblo ritual. There are frequent references in pueblo ethnographies to mythic and ceremonial journeys to and from the north and the middle place on sacred roads. These roads are metaphors as Ortiz states: `Road' translates as 'channel for life's breath' in Tewa. They speak of `life-breath openings' and `life-giving channels.' Every individual has a road of life that may be `cut short' at any time (Ortiz 1989). The Tewa mural paintings of San Juan depict these life-breath openings as shown in Figure 10.

Figure 10.   Tewa mural painting from San Juan depicting the "Installation ceremony of a Winter Man." Life breath openings and life giving channels are depicted along with *roadrunner tracks* on top of a cornmeal trail. (After Parsons, 1929:112)

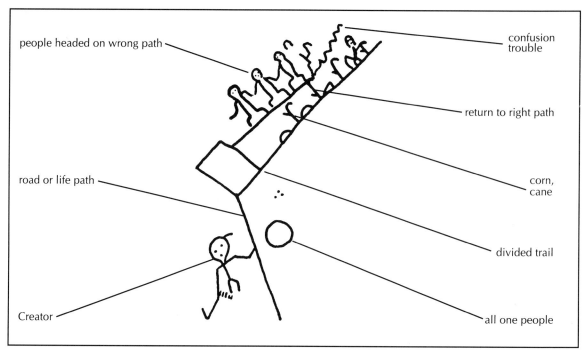

people headed on wrong path

confusion
trouble

return to right path

road or life path

corn,
cane

divided trail

Creator

all one people

Figure 11.   Hopi Prophesy Rock, Third Mesa, Hopi , Arizona. (After Martineau, 1973:116)

A graphic example that uses pueblo metaphors is the Hopi life plan petroglyph located on Third Mesa in Arizona (Figure 11). Hopi spokesman, Thomas Banyacya, has publicly explained the symbols on this panel many times over the years, giving the following interpretation:

> To the left is the Creator, with the life plan or trail. The circle represents all one people, no end, a circle. The Hopi path is divided. The three circles are the three past worlds. The corn plant is shown four times and is incorporated with the cane and a person leaning on it to symbolize old age. Together, the corn and cane symbolize everlasting life. Many people took the false path. The zigzag line is that of going back and forth (like water) in confusion and trouble. But there is still a pathway back down to the Hopi way. The last figure is the Creator holding the corn symbol for everlasting life. [4]

METONYMY

Metonymy is similar to metaphor, except that only a small part of a metaphor is used to represent the whole. It has been shown how corn and its life cycle are used as a metaphor for human life cycles. Metonymies are abbreviations of a whole metaphor or even a synopsis of a concept. By using the part, the whole is evoked in one's mind. In Christian religion, the symbol of a fish is a metonymy of the larger metaphor of "allowing Jesus into one's life." It is a symbol for the spiritual world that lies under the world of appearances. The fish represents the life-force surging up from within. It is grounded in the common knowledge of fishermen, who were among the first disciples of Jesus. He said, "Follow me, I will make you fishers of men." Johnson and Lakoff (1980:40) state:

> The conceptual systems of cultures and religions are metaphorical in nature. Symbolic metonymies are critical links between everyday experience and the coherent metaphorical system that characterize religions and cultures. Symbolic metonymies that are grounded in our physical experience provide an essential means of comprehending religious and cultural concepts.

Religious iconography is the most expressive form of a culture's metaphors and strives to present them in a way that conveys meaning to the culture. It defines the myth that defines the culture. When one looks at Pueblo iconography, one is looking at metonymies that bring to mind many of the Pueblos' elaborate cosmological concepts and cultural metaphors.

The metaphors of the Pueblo Indians, as well as those of other Indian tribes, are grounded in animal/nature experience. Pueblo knowledge of wildlife and other natural phenomena is a rich source of common experience and is drawn upon for metaphors to describe human activities. Animal activities are used as metaphors because they are common knowledge. The example given below of a deer track is a familiar image to any culture that has hunters. To a hunter, variations in the deer track can signify whether the animal is running or walking. If the track is grouped with other varied tracks, one can tell which are older and heavier, and which are younger and lighter. To a good hunter, animal tracks tell much about the animals, the direction and conditions in which they are traveling and their experiences along the way. Tracks convey this information cross-culturally and speak to the common knowledge of all hunters in any society.

Animal tracks found in petroglyphs are metonymies of the animal itself as a metaphor. The animals are metaphors used to represent people, while their tracks are ideal metaphors for expressing the activities, travel, battles or other conditions of people's lives.

In Plate 1, the photograph of a deer track shows dew claw marks. These marks only appear when a deer is running or fleeing.

Plate 1 also shows a pueblo petroglyph using the same track. It is found in sequence with a mountain lion print. In real-life experience, this would indicate a predator/prey relationship. Both tracks are going in the same direction, the lion track right behind the deer track. Together, they convey the action of the deer fleeing from a predator.

But more information has been added. The predator/prey petroglyph employs the repetition of the symbols to suggest a sequence of events. The mountain lion print is placed a second time, in front of the deer track. Simple deduction would conclude by this positioning that the mountain lion pursued the deer and overcame it.

But further investigation of the use of rock-incorporation as another symbol brings another conclusion to mind. The large crack running diagonally across the path of the two primary characters has been pecked-over and widened to emphasize its importance as part of the story. Beyond the crack is a single deer track, positioned well beyond the mountain lion print. Together the sequence of symbols tells the story of the predator chasing the prey, and the prey escaping across an obstacle (canyon or river) of some kind, with the predator unable to follow. The episode is more clearly illustrated in the drawing of Figure 12.

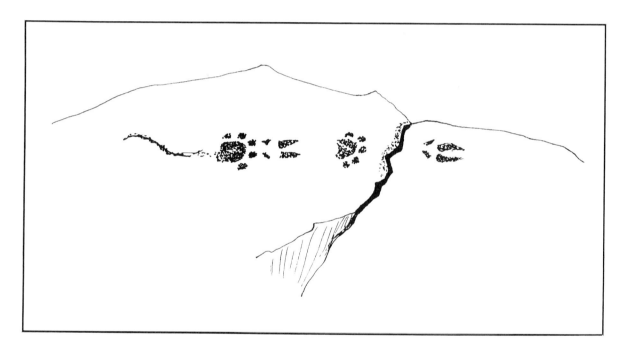

Figure 12.   Drawing of petroglyph with deer and mountain lion tracks from Los Lunas.

This panel is a classic example of use of the metonymy—animal tracks—in referring to the metaphor of a predator chasing prey; the concept of pursuing/fleeing, grounded in the common knowledge of all hunters cross-culturally. The predator/prey relationship in symbols is used frequently by Indian people as a metaphor for dangerous and life-threatening experiences with their enemies. This Anasazi petroglyph panel uses the predator/prey, pursuing/fleeing metaphor to describe the danger, the terror, the close encounter and the miraculous escape of someone from a mortal enemy. Note the use of lack-of space to illustrate "close encounter" with the enemy and wide space to show a "margin of safety." A diagram of the sequence of interpretation of this panel with the interpretative elements positioned as they are in the figure would look like this:

Metaphoric image	= lion print/deer print	lion print /crack	deer print
metonymy for	= lion/deer	lion/.....canyon.....deer	
common knowledge	= predator/prey	predator/.....canyon.....prey	
interpretation	= enemy/victim	enemy/.....canyon.....victim escaped	

At La Cienega, deer tracks occur as shown in Figure 13. This panel gives an account of both large and small deer fleeing down the side of the cliff. At the bottom, one track is portrayed inside a "shelter," and the dew claws are not indicated. This represents "standing still or relaxing." The entire panel uses the metaphor of deer fleeing down from above, to shelter, to show people seeking safety, perhaps below the mesa in the house ruins located there. The Indian author has drawn upon common knowledge of deer tracks to indicate fleeing and standing still, and the contrast of flight and safety. Both adults and children are portrayed metaphorically in the variation of size of deer prints.

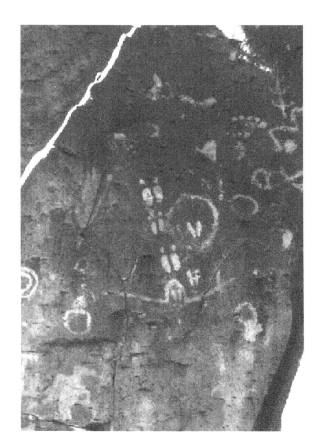

Figure 13.   Petroglyph of deer prints from the cliff face at La Cienega.

A Navajo panel in Largo Canyon, New Mexico (Figure 14) uses the same metonymy. In this panel, the combination of lion and deer tracks represents the U.S. Army (lion) pursuing the Navajos (deer) fleeing through Canyon del Muerto during the Kit Carson Campaign of 1863-64 (Martineau 1973:95-97).

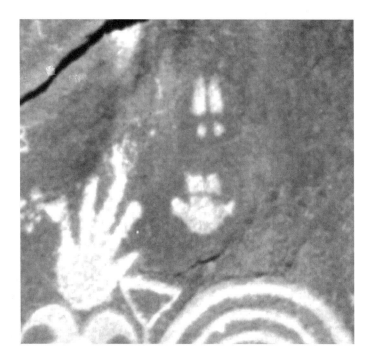

Figure 14. Petroglyph of deer and mountain lion prints found in the Navajo panel in Largo Canyon.

It has been shown how animal tracks can be metonymies referring to a specific metaphor that expresses a human condition or experience. Bird tracks are also metonymies and each species is easily identifiable by its track, which carries with it a specific set of attributes. These attributes are common knowledge among Pueblo tribes. Different birds play different roles in Pueblo mythology and religious iconography. Birds with attributes to help bring rain are distinguished from birds that compete for food or those that are helpful to hunters or those that are protective or informative to man. On one level, different birds play out parts in human drama to bring about balance in the universe. On another level, the birds may represent aspects of the human psyche that are best illustrated with metaphor.

Dumarest (1919:167), among others, has pointed out that to the Keresan people, the turkey, the crow, the eagle, the roadrunner, and the snake are represented by these tracks:

crow   turkey   eagle   roadrunner   snake

A photograph of a deer print that shows the dew claw marks that indicate the deer was running.

Rio Grande style petroglyph of deer and mountain lion prints, Los Lunas, New Mexico.

PLATE 1

Quadrupeds with heads and tails attached along with a shaman and shield figure. A warrior is depicted in an ambush posture. This panel is from Cottonwood Creek of Nine Mile Canyon, Utah. (Photo by Vernon E. Bush)

PLATE 2

The characteristics of each bird are important in Keresan mythology and are employed in their altars and mural paintings. As a metonymy, each refers to a metaphor for those aspects that keep the universe in balance.

Crow tracks are distinguished by their fourth rear toe. Crows' attributes include being in competition with man for food, but at times they are intelligent allies to man for religious purposes. Crow tracks in association with corn have been used by the Navajo to represent the act of destroying food, as in Figure 5 to emphasize the destruction of the piled-up corn. The common knowledge of the crow's relationship to corn is a metaphor to convey the act of Kit Carson's soldiers destroying the Navajo's corn supply and food source (Martineau 1973:101). Crow tracks may have a different metaphoric association to the pueblo, as we will see in the forthcoming chapters. To the Hopi, the crows in flocks are similar to the dark clouds that bring rain. They are associated with the kachinas with whom Crow Mother plays a major role. At Cochiti, the crow sometimes represents drought or witchcraft.

Turkey tracks are distinguished by having only three toes. It is common knowledge that turkeys depend upon the leadership of the older males to take care of the whole flock and lead it to water and to food. They are generous and giving in nature. Their tracks are important, metaphorically speaking, to indicate where to go when in need of food or water. Turkey tracks are commonly used in Rio Grande petroglyphs to indicate the direction of travel to a place of mutual interest, depending on the context or subject matter within the panel. The metaphor utilizes the common knowledge that the turkey tracks "will lead" to something or somewhere of importance.

Eagle claws are common among all tribes to represent the power of a bird whose domain is the highest reaches of the sky, and whose skill in hunting is paramount. The eagle is of utmost importance in religious iconography. It is the eagle's feathers that are used in curing rites, ceremonial attire, and in sacred fetishes. Their tracks are drawn in Keresan Pueblo altars to signify the sacred aspects of this bird and its role in pueblo cosmology.

The roadrunner (also referred to as chaparral cock) tracks in Eastern Pueblo and Zuni iconography are associated with courage and protection against enemies. The roadrunner has always been admired for his bravery, swiftness, and courage. He can kill and eat snakes, outruns most predators and leaves a track with two toes in each direction that makes his direction of travel ambiguous. The roadrunner track as a metaphor conveys the ideas of courage, bravery and the ability to confuse one's enemies. Figure 15 shows its use with a mountain lion track and conveys the opposite idea of the previously mentioned predator/prey relationship found in the lion/deer track combination. This figure shows the relationship of pursuer (mountain lion) in retreat from his prey (roadrunner).[5]

The symbols in this panel are metonymies for the animals-as-metaphors that represent the power of a warrior, who, like the roadrunner, is able to deter pursuit by his enemies. The interpretation of this petroglyph is consistent with Zuni ritual activities that entail wearing roadrunner feathers in an X formation inside their moccasins, or tied in their hair, to enhance their ability to confuse or deter their enemies in pursuit.[6]

25

Figure 15. Petroglyph of mountain lion and road-runner prints from San Diego Mountain, Southern Rio Grande area. (Photo from James Bain's collection, Laboratory of Anthropology/Museum of Indian Arts & Culture, Santa Fe).

To the Keresan Pueblos, the roadrunner is also important in protecting the souls of the dead along their pathway, when they come out from the underworld. Tracks of the roadrunner are marked along a symbolic corn meal trail to confuse witches and evil spirits and prevent them from accompanying souls on their journeys. Figure 16 is an illustration by Dumarest (1919) showing the use of several bird tracks in an "Altar for the Dead" from Cochiti Pueblo.

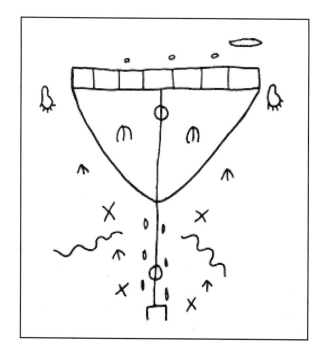

Figure 16. Bird and animal tracks identified by Dumarest in a sketch of an Altar for the Dead at Cochiti. (After Dumarest, 1919:167)

The Tewa also employ the roadrunner track for protection against enemies and witches. Figure 10 portrays the roadrunner tracks along the 'life-breath' road, and again in Figure 17, the roadrunner tracks are depicted along the life road trail.

Figure 17.   Tewa mural of the Kosa altar ceremony from San Juan, showing the roadrunner tracks on a cornmeal trail. (After Parsons 1929:126)

Bird and animal tracks are often metonymies for clans and depending upon the context of the other symbols in the panel, they may be interpreted as the metaphoric attributes applied either to a person or to a clan as a clan signature. The context of other symbols in a panel is necessary to determine how to interpret a bird or animal track as a clan symbol or a metonymy for the actual animal/metaphor.

Human tracks contain information about the human condition and status. They are metonymies for the person as a whole. A bare foot is associated with several conditions besides that of being without sandals or moccasins. The meaning of a bare foot is derived from the act of stripping down for battle, to take off all encumbering articles of clothing; travel packs, leather shirts or extraneous gear, and be streamlined for battle. The common phrase used by many tribes is "stripped for battle." The bare foot symbol refers to this phrase as a metaphor for battle when used with war or battle symbols. Bare feet indicate the bare essentials, the naked truth, the most basic relationship. Bare footprints are discussed further in Chapter 4. Human tracks can distinguish who went in one direction, and who returned in another direction. Large footprints alongside small footprints naturally convey the idea of both adults and children.

The positioning of human tracks signifies various meanings:

meet   depart   stayed   trail

Indian people use animals and their behavior as metaphors to convey concepts for human activities and emotions. Hundreds of animal tales are recorded in Indian oral traditions in which animals represent human personalities and behavior. It logically follows that the descendants of the Anasazi also depicted animals and animal tracks in the petroglyph panels to metaphorically describe the activities of humans. Human tracks focus more closely on the immediate condition of humans, but, together, metaphors and metonymies using animals and their tracks form a large part of the pictographic communication system under discussion. Another significant component within this code system involves the use of metaphoric animals with symbols attached or added. These images then become vehicles, for conveying more information, more efficiently, within a single container. An animal with symbols added can convey more information within its metaphor than many animals and strings of symbols portrayed independently. Thus, the strategy of saving space and time by combining several symbols to convey compact information is the incentive behind "sign vehicles" to be discussed next.

SIGN VEHICLES

The "goat" or horned quadruped is a neutral symbol that is used as a sign vehicle to display information about people, travel, conditions, and encounters. It does not represent a mythical animal, deity or important source of food. It appears throughout the continent, and is used by many diversified cultural groups, because of its non-association to a specific game animal. Rather, it is a generic symbol used to convey information by means of body posture and symbol add-ons. The quadruped in this context is not a clan symbol, beast god, power animal, or deity. There are no metaphorical attributes assigned to quadrupeds. They simply are combinations of symbols that collectively relate the conditions, lateral movements, and descriptions of a given topic, usually people. There are examples of the versatility of the quadruped as a sign vehicle throughout the petroglyphic record of all Indian tribes (Martineau 1973:46-67).

Keresan social organization contain no goat or mountain sheep clans. They do have on record the antelope and elk clans, (Lange 1959) that are easy to identify when used as clan symbols in the petroglyphs. The horns of antelope, deer, elk are distinctly different from each other. The quadrupeds under discussion in this book that are found in La Cienega and outlying areas of the Rio Grande Valley do not have "species identifying" horns that would suggest an actual animal.

Questions have always arisen as to why the use of quadrupeds is so profuse around the country and particularly the Southwest. Many well-meaning theories suggest the abundance of desert goats or mountain sheep that may have existed before historical time. Plate 2 is erroneously labeled as "hunting scenes" because of a fixation on species identification or a literal rather than symbolic interpretation.

The quadrupeds portrayed in this panel are all attached by lines from the nose of each to the other's tail or back. This suggests a lineage or blood relationship. Each band has young ones included. A shaman is also portrayed as a leader of the band. A shield-figure stands ready to defend his "herd" of family relatives. These *people* are being attacked by another tribe. Note the mutilated human body (body half), and the position of the warrior, in an "ambush" posture. A "hunting magic" or "mountain sheep" theory would not fit within the context of shield figures, human death and mutilation.

Hunting magic theories do not explain why, if such animals existed in abundance, they are not found in the same proportions within the native oral traditions, myths and legends, as clan names or power animals, as might be expected in comparison to their widespread use in the petroglyphs. The reason is that they are used as sign vehicles to illustrate human activities. The attention of the reader should be drawn away from the "species" identification and instead focus on the quadruped as a "symbol."

The horned quadruped is a neutral animal that allows for variations in body shape and appendages to express various human activities and conditions . The quadruped, when broken down into component parts, can have a repertoire of information contained within each variation of a body part. A simple breakdown of the quadruped is found in

Figure 18.   Quadrupeds with backward feet from Indian Creek, Utah. (Photo by Mark Sink)

Chart 1. It is the Western viewpoint (etic) that insists on categorizing all quadrupeds as representations of actual animals. The ethnographic record (emic) does not support it.

    The heads point in the direction of travel. The curved horns are lines that represent the hand sign for a general movement or direction of travel, uninterrupted, from point A to point B. The two lines, when parallel, indicate an open space. This is to say, "nothing there" or "open" which means "good" in terms of traveling space. When the space between the horns is filled in, it means "something there" and usually refers to obstruction of some kind. An irregular line, as opposed to a smooth curved line, denotes a rough journey, associated with difficulties. Martineau (1973) gives many examples of these basic line variations and their equivalence in sign language.

    The bodies incorporate a variety of different symbols to indicate geographical formations and landscapes in which people (not goats) are traveling. These variations include general places, such as valleys, hills, and canyons. The legs describe something about what the people did, as in "staying," "leaving," "avoiding," "standing firm" or "resisting conflict," "giving up," and "departing".

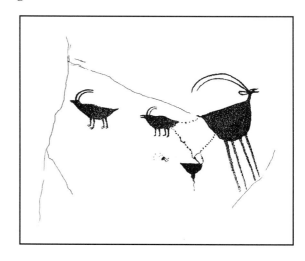

Figure 19.   Quadrupeds with symbol incorporations in their bodies, feet, horns, heads, and legs. Ink drawing of this Anasazi petroglyph from Navajo National Monument.

The feet vary in shape and denote something about travel, such as whether the people left a trail or if they went and returned (backward feet). Figure 18 shows an example of a quadruped with backward feet indicating that he returned.

When reference to big-horned sheep, desert sheep, or mountain goats is intended in Indian pictography, the image is realistic and not abstracted or suggestive. Nor is it inclusive of added-on symbols. In Indian oral traditions, especially in myths, *animals represent people.* Animals and people are interchangeable. People are portrayed as animals in order to emphasize certain attributes and allow for a clearer distinction between characters. Thus the quadruped is suggestive in order to emphasize the attributes and give clarity to what human actions are being conveyed in the petroglyph panels. It is in true character and consistency with Indian literature and art to utilize an animal form to express the activities of people.

Figure 20.   Quadruped from La Cienega with symbol incorporation appearing as continuous legs.

Figure 19 portrays the use of quadrupeds with altered horns, bodies, and feet to express different ideas pertaining to the direction and condition of travel, the geographical area the people were traveling and what their concerns were. The use of elongated legs may suggest the length or continuous travel. The use of the deep bowl shape body suggests a valley. The curved horns over the entire body indicate the journey across the entire valley. The eyes and ears depicted on this quadruped indicate "looking" and "listening" as they traveled. The other two quadrupeds are moving in the opposite direction. Both have "foot prints" leading to them from the larger quadruped. Both smaller ones incorporate the "canyon" symbol in their body and they have different "feet" that represent different ideas specific to each one. Neither have "ears" or "eyes" that is a detail important in the story.

When an animal or bird is portrayed realistically, without symbol add-ons, or abstractions, by its very nature it is limited to a direct "species identification." A realistic image does not function as a symbol for an idea or concept. Even clans are identified by

Figure 21. Quadruped from La Cienega with the symbol incorporations in the body and tail which wraps around the top of the rock.

abstracted or simplified *symbols*. Yet most of the current literature addresses quadrupeds as representations of "species" rather than symbols, without asking instead, "what do they mean?" The quadruped's use in a symbol system for transmitting information is of great importance if one is to try to understand the meanings of the petroglyph panels.

At La Cienega, several quadrupeds are found with unusual depictions of body parts and with spatial placement to indicate certain aspects of their meaning as symbols. The symbol add-ons are evident in Figure 20, which depicts the legs in a continuous arc from front to back.

Figure 21 is a quadruped with the tail as a symbol of a "trail" or "pathway" that originates from behind the rock and wraps around, over the edge and down to the body. The body of the quadruped incorporates the "bowl" symbol that is reference to a "valley" or low geographical area. The legs incorporate the sharp-angled symbol that indicates "standing firm." This sign vehicle is expressing, in general, a movement of people "coming over the ridge, into the valley and standing their ground."

Figure 22 is an example of the quadruped showing direction of movement down into a canyon. The animal is in an inclined position. The body has incorporated the "canyon" symbol. This sign vehicle contains a portion of information within the context of a large panel of symbols that tells a complicated story.

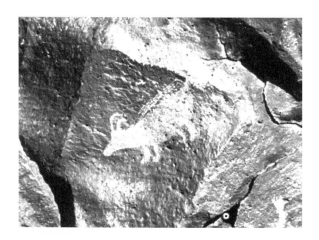

Figure 22. Quadruped from La Cienega with symbol incorporation of the "canyon" shape and body position of traveling down an incline. Together they suggest moving into a canyon.

Figure 23 portrays a quadruped with two heads. Each half is a mirror image of itself. The idea of "twins," or "brothers" may be portrayed here.

Figure 23.   Quadruped from La Cienega with two heads.

There are also portraits of Spanish horsemen with the horses exaggerated in different ways to add information about the Spaniards and their horses, where they are going or what they are doing. Figure 24 also shows a Spanish horseman riding a "branded" horse.

Figure 24.   Petroglyph from La Cienega depicting a Spanish horseman on a "branded " horse.

Figure 25 shows a Spanish horseman. The front legs of the horse are raised to indicate "stepping up." The center leg is the rider's, that reaches to the ground to indicate "stepping down." Together, these symbols indicate the action of "mounting and dismounting" in reference to the horseman's abilities, which may have been a new phenomenon to the Indian.

Figure 25. Petroglyph in La Cienega of a Spanish horseman with the body posture of "stepping up." An extra leg is added to depict "stepping down." Together they convey the ability of the Spanish rider to mount and dismount the horse.

Figure 26. Petroglyph in La Cienega of a Spanish horseman on a horse with "boots" on, a statement about the Spanish practice of shoeing their horses.

The horse in Figure 27 is incorporated into the "bowl" or "saddle" symbol to suggest the "saddle" in the landscape just in front of the panel. The crisscrossed symbol represents pens or rooms that are associated with the horse because they are attached to its tail. The horse and rider are oriented at an upward slant that indicates the direction of some actual ruins of stone-walled sheep pens located in the saddle between the hills just in front of the panel. The context of the site, together with the symbol incorporations, suggests that this panel is referring to the Spanish horseman using the natural saddle in the landscape as a site for his sheep pens.

Figure 27. Petroglyph in La Cienega located at the edge of the rock outcropping overlooking a shallow basin or "saddle" in the mesa formation along with the ruins of stone walled sheep pens. The Spanish rider is headed in the direction of the "saddle" area. His horse has the symbol incorporation of the geographical terrain ahead.

Figure 28 is the geographical area in front of the horse and rider, showing the actual saddle area with stone walled sheep pens.

Figure 28. A view looking back at the basin with the sheep pens and the rock outcropping with the petroglyph site in the background.

The horse, as with the quadruped, has had its body parts exaggerated to better describe different aspects about the horse and the Spanish rider. When the horse was introduced to the indigenous cultures of North America during the 1500s, its body shape was easily incorporated into the symbol system. The Plains Indians exaggerated body parts to emphasize speed, power, fleetness of foot, great distances of travel and more, whereas the Pueblo Indians incorporated other symbols into the horse to refer to specific activities taking place with the horse and rider. The horse has been used as a sign vehicle to express the Spanish rider and the terrain he is passing through.

CONCLUSION

Understanding and explaining Indian pictography requires a semiotic approach. Animal or bird metaphors draw upon culturally specific attributes combined with animal/nature experiences that are grounded in a common knowledge. Animals-as-metaphors utilize the animal form by exaggeration or modification, in an endless variety of forms to convey specific concepts. Indian pictography is a graphic symbol system well established that utilizes the different attributes of each animal as ideograms by combining and recombining a limited number of symbols to convey complicated meanings.

Metaphors are culturally specific and draw upon the experiences of a culture, which in the case of Indians, is highly contextual. Metonymies are found primarily in reference to a metaphor, clan or mythical figure. They may refer to common knowledge that is cross-cultural and not necessarily high in context. Sign vehicles are different from metonymies or metaphors in that they are not referent to, or limited to one specific animal. They are made up of unlimited variations of animal, human, bird, or insect combinations. Sign vehicles are low context symbols that convey information that is not culturally specific but that draws directly upon common knowledge, and body language. Martineau has consistently pointed out that Indian sign language is a reference source for symbols attached to sign vehicles. Body posture and spatial positioning are aspects of sign language that can be applied to a semiotic study of Indian pictography, especially sign vehicles. Indian sign language draws upon metaphors that are grounded in the physiology of the human body as a personal perspective, and natural phenomenon including animal/man relationships as a global perspective. Knowledge of Indian sign language greatly enhances one's ability to interpret Indian symbols, metonymies and metaphors. Indian sign language has a direct relationship between thought and sign that, in effect, bypasses language and cultural barriers.

American Indian sign language was recommended by early scholars as a communication system worth investigating in order to better understand Indian world views. Clark (1885) stressed the importance for every cavalry officer and man on the western frontier to learn Indian sign language in order to better understand the Indian. Clark writes:

> "Educated as the Indians are by nature and drawing many of their metaphors and comparisons from her abundant reservoirs, it is no wonder that one must know something of their lives to talk fluently and understand quickly. To become, in short, accomplished, one must train the mind to think like the Indians. " (Clark [1885] 1982:17)

In this century, little attention has been given to American Indian sign language as a body of knowledge that is useful for petroglyph interpretation. In the 19th century, Mallery ([1893] 1972:421) stated: "The part of the pictographs which are the most difficult of interpretation is the one which the study of Indian sign language can elucidate." William Tomkins (1926) recognized the importance of American Indian sign language and wrote:

37

"All Indian languages are highly figurative [metaphorical] and poetic compared to ours, resembling the Chinese in its idiomatic construction, but I know of nothing that gives so complete an insight into the peculiarities of Indian thought and expression as does a thorough study of their universal sign language" (Tomkins [1926] 1968:91).

La Van Martineau (1973) undertook the study of petroglyphs, following these scholars' advice, and learned the American Indian sign language thoroughly. He has stated emphatically its importance in petroglyph interpretation because of the metaphors characteristic of Indian world views in contrast to those of the European thinkers. The following are examples of Indian metaphors, taken from Clark's sign language manual that are distinctly different from their usage in European culture.

<u>Divorce</u> in Indian sign language is expressed by the concept of being "thrown away." The concept is extended to mean "abandoned," "deserted," "displaced" or "forsaken." Divorce is to "throw away" one's spouse when he or she is no longer tolerated. The same concept is applied to a chief who has been deposed of his rank. His tribe may "throw him away." **<u>Marry</u>** is to "trade for" or "to purchase" and is expressed in those terms. The concept of **<u>jealous</u>** is to "elbow to one side." This gesture represents the idea of envy and insecurity. For the concept **to die**, the Indian draws on the metaphor of "going under" or being "knocked over." Clark (1885:150) states: "There is a strong faith in a happy hereafter and as a consequence they do not agonize over death." In contrast, the European culture defines **<u>die</u>** as "pass away, become senseless, stop living, suffer agony of death, cease to exist, end."

When asked about **God**, Clark reports that the Indian metaphor is "The Great Mystery" and in concept is synonymous with *medicine*. This concept is gestured by adding the two, "medicine" and "great" together. In European cultures, **religion** is generally separate from medicine and the merging of the two is relatively uncommon. The English dictionary defines **medicine** as "the science and art of diagnosing, treating, curing, and preventing disease, relieving pain and preserving health." A common metaphor "to take one's medicine" is given in reference to the enduring of just punishment. It goes without saying that a mental image of a medical doctor would not include religious iconography. Instead, the media portray a doctor as a person in a white lab coat with a stethoscope around his neck.

The medicine man found in most Indian pictography is portrayed quite differently, with the combination of two metaphors. A **medicine man** or shaman has both "strength" or "religious powers" and "healing" abilities. He is represented with symbolism that combines both concepts. Figure 29 shows a Pueblo petroglyph that has a medicine man among other figures. The attribute of *strength* is denoted by the horns, and *healing* by the plant held in one hand.

Another reason for studying American Indian sign language is for the comparative value of understanding the structural format that is found in both Indian pictography and Indian sign language. From their structure it is possible to gain a better understanding of how the two systems work in that on the whole they are metaphoric, nonlinear, and employ

Figure 29.   Petroglyph of a Medicine Man from Las Agules pueblo ruin site west of La Cienega. The central figure has horns to depict "strength" and is holding a plant to indicate herbal remedies or "medicine".

the use of spatial syntax. The following are characteristics of Indian sign language:

1.   It contains ionic or pantomimic signs, which are those signs that reproduce by gesture, in "air drawings," the action or object being described. About 98% of sign language is composed of these signs and accounts for its "universality." (West 1968)

2.   The remaining 2% are lexical signs that are specific symbols and can be categorized with more consistency. Only 20-40% of these signs were shared among the Plains Indian groups that were studied.

3.   Also in the lexical category are determinative signs that assign qualities or characteristics to their referents. Determinative signs modify the basic signs being gestured by denoting repetition, size, quality, importance, and status. The change of positioning in relation to the signer may indicate time; past, present or future.

Sign language does not follow a syntactic order or pattern of linguistic style specific to any one Indian language. It has its own unique non-linear format called spatial syntax. As a true language, it contains the following characteristics:

Simultaneity; i.e., when two or more different signs are produced together to form one meaning.

Reversibility; i.e., when gesture signs are reversed to show the opposite in meaning.

Directionality; i.e., when gesture signs are positioned in space relative to the signer and the ground, or with the hand positioned in different ways to add meaning.

When gesture signs are grouped or combined to convey one single meaning, the process is called *agglutination*. Agglutinating signs allows limitless extensions of basic signs and the invention of new ways to express a concept for which one single sign does not suffice. The most common utilization of agglutination is the forming of a string of signs which, taken simultaneously, transmits one idea (Skelly:1979).

The structural format of spatial syntax and agglutination can be identified within the Indian picture writing system. Simultaneity, reversibility, and directionality are all elements of a formal structure that has been applied to the interpretation of the panels discussed in this book. Spatial syntax relies on the proximity of symbols to communicate the whole event. The mountain lion/deer sequence, for example, illustrates the dynamics of spatial variation.

Even though records of the Pueblos using sign language are very few, evidence of their knowledge of the system exists to this day.[7] Sign language is still used in situations where information is discussed that is appropriate only for initiated participants and not for the general public. Sign language is still being used between young children and grandparents, in the pueblos, in situations where the young children have been taught English instead of the native language and their grandparents do not know English well.

A comprehensive study of Pueblo Indian sign language is needed to better complete a comparison with the Pueblo Indian picture writing. It is the internal structure which is of the most concern and which will be used for comparison at this point. Other sign languages around the world—including Chinese, Old World deaf, American and Monastic sign languages—have the same basic structure as that outlined above. It is very probable that the same structure, found in the Plains Indian version of sign language, is comparable to the Pueblo Indian version. It is the visual dynamics of sign language that are of concern and applied to the petroglyphic analysis in this book.

The Charts following the last chapter contain headings that include both emic and etic points of view. The spatial syntax and body posture information inherent in sign language is utilized in an etic analysis of the panels. The mythic constituent units and cultural context from the specific culture is utilized in the emic analysis. Together the charts evaluate the petroglyphs in a more holistic manner.

ENDNOTES

1. Alfonsas Savickas in *The Concept of Symbol in the Psychology of C. G. Jung*, Resch Verlag Innsbruck, 1979, has summarized several views regarding the differences between a sign and a symbol: "a sign is more directed at the rational and intellectual part of man, the symbol makes its appeal upon the irrational and emotional side (F. Dillistone 1927); a sign is more linked with time and place dimensions, the symbol is not limited to such details (S. Langer 1951:58-61); a sign is an expression of something known, the symbol is the best possible expression for something relatively unknown (C.G.Jung:1960:515); the sign is designated more by a definite physical individuality, the symbol is more general and less exact in its direction (F. Kaulbach; 1954:101); the symbol fulfills the function of the sign (Wisse;1958:195). Langer considers sign as a generic term to include both signal and symbol. The difference between sign and symbol is considered to be gradual and not categorical. (Wisse;31). All symbols are also signs but not all signs are symbols."

Firth (1973:73-75) gives the following definitions:

An Index - where a sequential relation is inferred.
A Sign - an indication of something but not classified as a symbol for something.
A Signal - emphasis in a sign is upon consequential action.
An Icon - a sensory likeness-relation is intended.
Symbol - where a sign has a complex series of associations (Firth;1973:73-75).

2. Basso (in Spradley,1972:346) states "The application of anatomical terminology to motorized vehicles illustrates an aspect of semantic extension that is clearly apparent at the level of the set, but that goes undetected if we focus on the individual terms in isolation. Thus a typical `atomistic' interpretation - operating strictly at the word level and failing to consider the internal structure of the lexical set as a whole - would not disclose that together with individual terms a classificatory scheme had also been extended." He lists in his Table 19.1 Western Apache Anatomical Terms With Extended Meanings:

Anatomical Terms (re: man)	Extended meanings (re: auto)
shoulder	front fender
hand + arm	front wheels, tires
chin + jaw	front bumper
foot, feet	rear wheels, tires
face	area from windshield to bumper
forehead	front portion of cab
nose	hood
back	bed of truck
hip = buttock	rear fender
mouth	gas tank opening
eyes	headlights
veins	electrical wiring
entrails, guts	all machinery under hood
liver	battery
stomach	gas tank
heart	distributor
lung	radiator
intestine	radiator hoses
fat	grease

3. An article entitled "The Great North Road: a Cosmographic Expression of the Chaco Culture of New Mexico," produced by the Solstice Project 1988, Anna Sofaer, Michael P. Marshall, and Rolf M. Sinclair describe the complex series of roads radiating out from the Chaco Canyon National Monument. The interpretation of these roads as arteries connecting communities for trade, transportation of goods and materials is generally accepted but does not explain why some end so abruptly or run in sections of two or four parallel. Many do not lead to outlying communities, but rather to sparsely populated areas. However, in the ethnographic record, many references are made to roads for the spirits of the dead returning to the Sipapu. The Zuni have prayers and chants telling of their emergence and migration to the middle place and reference is made to four parallel roads.

4. Presented by Thomas Banyacaya at the World Conference of Indigenous People's Education, Vancouver, 1987. A similar interpretation is given in Martineau (1973:116)

5. Schaafsma (1989:253-269) concludes also that the use of the roadrunner track in pictography is more symbolic than for hunting magic. Though Schaafsma has demonstrated a predator/prey relationship, in her Fig.11.3, the tracks are clearly reversed, and show the "prey" chasing the "predator." In other words, this is an enemy/warrior relationship, the warrior confusing or scaring the enemy into retreat.

6. Parsons relates her observations of pueblo sign language in rituals and dances in her book "Pueblo Indian Religion" pages 390-393.

7. Parsons (1939:291) notes: "Feathers of the bird of courage, the Chaparral cock, are worn in moccasins or hair by Zuni scalp-kickers in order to gain courage....(Stevenson) [1904:584]. Again the feathers may serve against pursuit."

3
WATER JAR BOY MYTH

It comes alive
It comes alive, alive, alive
In the North Mountain
The lion comes alive
In the North Mountain, comes alive.
With this the prey animal
Will have power to attract deer, antelope;
Will have power to be lucky.

_____Acoma poem

In this chapter, the myth Water Jar Boy, and the metaphors used to represent important concepts within the myth, are compared to the symbols in the petroglyph panel that can be identified in Eastern pueblo iconography. The petroglyph panel, so-called "Water Jar Boy", is located on the cliff face overlooking the ruin of La Cienega.

To understand the petroglyphs under discussion, the myth will be presented first. The origin of the myth appears to be Tewa. One version of this myth called "The Jug Boy," from the Hopi-Tewa village of Hano, was recorded by Voth (1905:55). The longer version, called "Water Jar Boy," was recorded by Elsie Clews Parsons (1926:193) in her "Tewa Tales." [1] Parsons recorded this myth from the Tewa and it also persists among the Hopi-Tewa descendants of Tewa immigrants. The Eastern Pueblo metaphors found in the myth help facilitate the identification of the symbols present in the petroglyph panel, with emphasis on the way in which mythical characters are portrayed in animal or bird form in a petroglyph to symbolize the attributes of the characters in a myth. The power of metaphor has been utilized in this myth to enhance our understanding of the very fundamental themes in Eastern Pueblo world views.

Animal and bird tracks are used as metonymies for animal metaphors. The animals themselves are used as metaphors for human aspirations, emotions, and social relationships. The myth is reprinted in full for the purpose of retaining the language and structure as it was recorded in the 1920s by Elsie Clews Parsons. The significant elements are bold-faced to help the reader identify the elements in the story that correspond to those symbols found in the petroglyph panel for the discussion that follows.

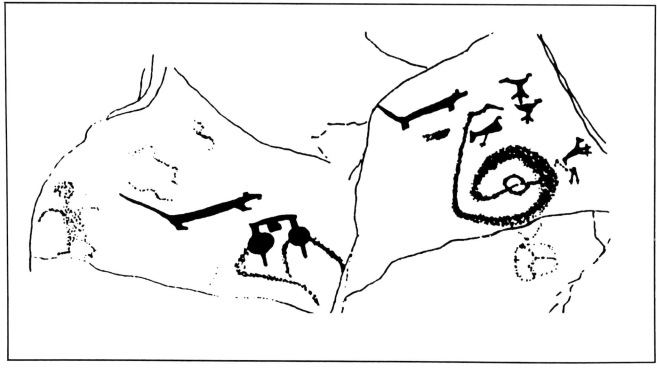

Figure 30.   Ink drawing of the entire Water Jar Boy petroglyph.

WATER JAR BOY

They were living at **Sikyat'ki**. There was a girl living there, a fine girl, and she did not want to **marry** any of the boys living there. After a while **boys in the other villages heard there was a fine girl living at Sikyat'ki but she did not want any boy.** Her mother was all the time making water jars. One day when her mother **was mixing clay and using one foot,** she was watching her mother. Her mother said she wanted to go for some water. "You can **keep on doing this for me,"** said her mother. So she (the girl) stepped on the mud and began to mix it with her foot on top of a flat stone. So she was **trying to mix the mud** for her mother. Somehow that **mud got into the girl**, it flew up. She felt it on her leg, but not higher up inside. Then her mother came back and asked her if she finished the mud.

"Yes," she said.

So her mother went on making the water jars.

After some days the girl felt something was moving in her belly, but she did not think anything about going to **have a baby**. She did not tell her mother. But it was growing and growing.

One day in the morning she was very sick. In the afternoon she **got the baby.** Then her mother knew (for the first time) that her daughter was going to have a baby. The mother was very angry about it; but after she looked at the baby, she saw it was not like a baby, she saw **it was a round thing with two things sticking out,** it was a little jar.

"Where did you get this?" said her mother.

The girl was just crying.

About that time the father came in. "Never mind, I am very glad she had a baby," he said. "But it is not a baby," said her mother.

Then the father went to look at it and saw it was **a little water jar.** After that he was very fond of that little jar.

"It is moving," he said.

Pretty soon the little water jar was growing. In twenty days it was big. It was able to go around with the children, and it could talk.

"Grandfather, take me outdoors, so I can look around," he said.

So every morning the grandfather would take him out and he would look at the children, and they were very fond of him and they found out he was a boy, **Sipe'geenu** (Tewa), Water Jar Boy. They found out from his talking.

About the time of year (December) it began to snow, and the men were going out to hunt rabbits, and Water Jar Boy wanted to go.

"Grandfather, could you take me down to the foot of the mesa, **I want to hunt rabbits."**

"Poor grandson, you can't hunt rabbits, you have no legs or arms."

" Well Grandfather," he said," I am very anxious to go. Take me anyway. You are too old and you can't kill anything."

His mother was crying because her boy had no legs or arms or eyes. But they used to feed him in his mouth (i.e. in the mouth of the jar).

So next morning his grandfather took him down to the south on the flat. Then he rolled along, and pretty soon he saw a rabbit track and he followed the track. Pretty soon the

45

rabbit ran out, and he began to chase it. Just before he got to the marsh there was a rock, and **he hit himself against it and broke and a boy jumped up.**

He was very glad his skin had been broken and that he was a boy, a big boy. He was wearing lots of beads around his neck and turquoise earrings, and a dance kilt and moccasins, and a buckskin shirt.

Then he chased the rabbit, he picked up a stick and ran. Pretty soon he killed it. Then he found another rabbit and chased again. He was a good runner. So **he killed four rabbits,** jackrabbits.

About that time the sun was setting, so he went home, **carrying the rabbits on his back.** His grandfather went down to the place where he had carried him and waited for him. While his grandfather was waiting there, somebody was coming. Then came a fine looking boy, but his grandfather did not know who it was.

"Did you see my grandson anywhere?" said the grandfather to that boy.

He said."No, I did not see your grandson anywhere."

"Well, I am sorry he is late."

"Well I did not see anybody anywhere" said the boy. His grandfather was looking so bad, the boy said." I am your grandson."

"No, you are just teasing me, my grandson is a round jar, with-out arms or legs," said the grandfather. He did not believe it was his grandson. But the boy said,"I am your grandson. I am telling you the truth. This morning you carried me down here. I went to look for rabbits near here. I found one and chased him just rolling along. Pretty soon I hit myself on a rock and my skin was broken and I came out of it and I am the very one who is your grandson, and you must believe me. " So he believed and they went home.

When they came back and the grandfather was bringing in a good-looking boy, the girl was ashamed. The grandfather said, "This is my grandson, this is Water Jar Boy, " and the grandmother asked how he became a boy, and he told them how it had happened to him, and they believed it. Then after that he went around with the boys. One time he said to his mother, **"Who is my father?" he said.** "I don't know," she said. He asked her again, "Who is my father?" But she just kept on crying and did not answer.

"Where is my father's home?" he asked. **She could not tell him.**

"Tomorrow I am going to find my father."

"You cannot find your father," she said. "I never go with any boys, so there is no place where you can look for your father."

But the boy said, "I have a father, I know where he is living, I am going to see him." The mother did not want him to go, but he wanted to go. So early next morning she fixed a lunch for him, and he went off to the southeast where they call the **spring Waiyu Powidi,** (Horse Mesa Point). He was coming close to that spring, he saw somebody walking a little way from the spring. He went up to him. It was a man. He asked the boy, "Where are you going?"

"I am going to this spring."

"Why are you going?"

"I am going there to see my father," he said.

"Who is your father?" said the man.

46

"Well, my father is living in this spring."
"You will never find your father."
"Well, I want to go into the spring, he is living inside it."
"Who is your father?" said the man again.
"Well, I think you are my father," said the boy.
"How do you know I am your father?" said the man.
"Well, I know you are my father." Then the man just looked at him, to scare him. The boy kept saying "You are my father." Pretty soon the man said, "Yes, I am your father. I came out of that spring to meet you," and he put his arm around the boy's neck. His father was very glad his boy had come, and he took him down inside of the spring. A lot of people were living down **inside of the spring,** women and girls. They all ran to the boy and put their arms around him because they were glad their child had come to their house. Thus the boy found his father and his aunts, too.

Well, the boy stayed there one night and next day he went back home and told his mother he had found his father. Then his mother got sick and she died. Then the boy said to himself, "No use for me to live with these people." So he left them and went to the spring. And there was his mother. That was the way he and his mother went to live with his father. His father was **Avaiyo pi'i** (Water Snake Red). He said he could not live with them over at Sikyat'ki. That was the reason he made the boy's mother sick so she died and "came over here to live with me," said his father. "Now we will live here together," said **Avaiyo** to his son. That's the way that boy and his mother went to the spring to live there.

Printed with permission from the American Folklore Society, from "**Tewa Tales**," by Elsie Clews Parsons, the American Folklore Society Memoirs, Vol. XIX, 1926,

The pueblo petroglyph panel entitled "Water Jar Boy" contains symbols that have little resemblance to the characters described in the oral version. When viewed in a metaphorical sense, however, the petroglyph panel, illustrated herein, can be shown to contain the very same elements and illustrate the same sequence of events found in the myth. By using the myth as a guide, the unusual symbols become meaningful and follow the mythical story line with remarkable consistency.

Figure 31.   Ink drawing of Water Jar Boy Panel 1.

Figure 32.   Ink drawing of Water Jar Boy Panel 2.

48

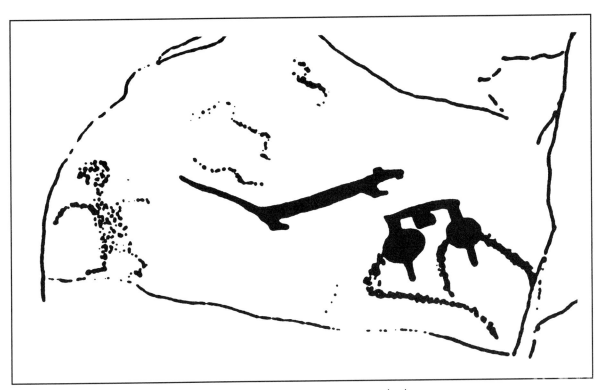

Figure 33.   Ink drawing of Panel 3 of the Water Jar Boy petroglyph.

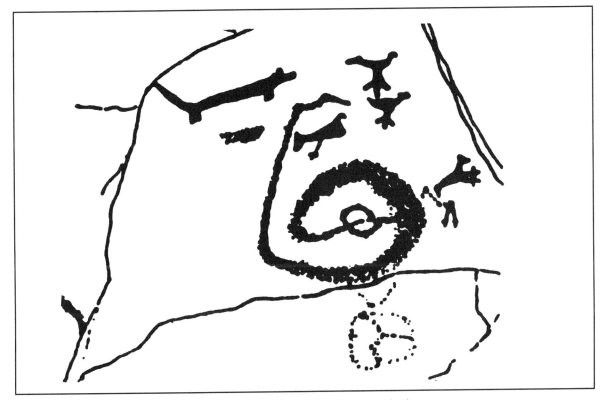

Figure 34.   Ink drawing of Panel 4 of the Water Jar Boy petroglyph.

49

SYMBOL IDENTIFICATION

The petroglyph panels associated with this myth are found in a series, reading from upper right to lower left across the cliff face above the site of La Cienega. These panels have been assigned numbers for easier reference; Panel 1 to the right and Panel 2 on the left as shown in Figures 31 and 32.

The beginning of the myth contains many aspects, or constituent units such as, a girl who did not want to marry any of the boys of her village; a supernatural conception; giving birth to a water jar; a boy growing up inside a water jar. These elements are expressed pictographically in the following way.

Panel 1 has flute players, more specifically identified as "wife hunters." These figures are shown with back packs, playing flutes, and having rabbit ears. These are all elements associated with courting, wooing and prolificacy having to do with "wife purchasing," (Martineau 1973:53), and as "a hunter and moccasin maker who in the tales appears with a buckskin on his back from which to make moccasins for a bride" (Parsons 1938:337). The name "Kokopelli," as commonly used for all kinds of flute players, comes from a mythical locust-like insect character who is able to bring rain and fertility for the people of Zuni. He is referred to in Hopi mythology as well. In Panel 1, the flute players are not insects with humped backs, but men with packs, playing flutes and walking in one direction. In pre-historic pueblo culture it was customary for young men to go "wife hunting" to other villages, carrying gifts for a bride and playing a flute to court her.

In the petroglyph panel, these figures are portrayed as phallic and "prolific as rabbits" as part of their appeal. They are easily identified by their human bodies, hands and feet, backpacks, and rabbit ears. In contrast, the insect, Kokopelli, has a hump that is a continuous part of his back with insect antenna and an insect head. He is found near La Cienega, at Cienegilla, but is very different from the flute players in this panel. A comparison is drawn between various flute players and insect-like Kokopellis in Chart 2.

Figure 35.   Two Flute players from Cienegilla with distinctly different backpacks.

50

In Figure 35 from Cienegilla, is an example of two distinctly different types of back packs. One is level along the top or brim that suggests a burden basket, while the other is rounded that is characteristic of a back pack. Neither type depicts "humped" backs, but rather vessels or packs carried on the back.

Careful attention to the details of the many variations of the flute player figure, can better determine the identity of these figures. It would be misleading to associate "agriculture," "rain" and a "fertile seed pack," concepts with this panel, as so often are associated with the insect Kokopelli. Symbol association with a female figure giving birth adds further evidence that these flute players are associated with wife hunting rather than with seed germination.

In contrast, Panel 2 has a figure playing a flute but not carrying a pack. The meaning symbolized by this figure has changed with the context. In the same panel is a second figure with a hump on his back and a phallus but not playing a flute. Each of these three figures is a variation of a flute player, having a specific meaning implied within the context of symbols around them and their role in the myth being represented.

In Panel 1 the five figures with ceremonial belts, packs (of bridal goods), flutes (for courting) and rabbit ears (prolificacy) are used in context with a figure (female) in a birthing position. The "birthing" position has characteristic flexed knees and out-spread legs, with a second image positioned below and between the legs. The symbol below the legs represents "what was born" and in this case it is something not clearly identifiable. Within the mythical context, the maiden is giving birth to a "round thing with two things sticking out." The petroglyph emphasizes two qualities of this "something" with two symbols. The first object is a circle with a dot inside, indicating a round thing with something in it, like a container of some kind. The second image has feet-like appendages that may represent the aspect of mobility in a human form.

In the story, the question remains: Who of the above males is the father? The petroglyph shows the "suitors" or "wife hunters" going their own way, in one direction. There are no figures turning back or "returning." A returning figure might indicate that he had been chosen by the maiden. This is an important detail from the standpoint of symbol analysis. The positioning and formation of these pack-carrying, flute-playing, wife-hunting suitors, traveling in one direction without returning, indicate a continuing search going away from home. There are no indications of a suitor touching or "being with her" to indicate a marriage or a relationship to the birth. Within the context of the myth, this question is a basic element in the story: "Who is my Father?" One can tell from the panel alone, that the suitors were not responsible for the birth.

The female figure in the petroglyph reinforces this theory by being portrayed wearing a horned headdress, which indicates extraordinary strength or powers. Horned figures are usually associated with shamans, or persons having strong "medicine." Male or female deities are portrayed in kiva art, (Dutton 1963, Hibben 1975) using horned headdresses that call attention to a special denotation of power or ability. Within the context of the myth, the horned female figure is identified as the maiden who gave birth

51

from a supernatural conception. Thus she has been elevated to the status of a deity. Several examples of the use of horns to portray deities or higher status individuals are given in Figure 36.

| Horns | Apache | Navajo | Pueblo | Pueblo |

Figure 36. Several examples of horned figures.

There are many stories in pueblo mythology that describe pregnancies from supernatural events. This supernatural conception is illustrated in Panel 2. The humped-back phallic figure near the top is positioned in association with two figures copulating. Further to the right is the *basic* symbol for "movement back and forth" $\wedge\!\!\wedge\!\!\wedge$, zigzag lines that have the extended meaning as lightning or bodies of water like a river, both of which move back and forth (Mallery [1893] 1972:642, Martineau 1973:101,103). The myth relates how the mud splashes up the maiden's leg, causing her to conceive and eventually give birth. Within the zigzag lines is a figure who's arms and legs are incorporated into each zigzag line. This incorporation of arm and leg with "movement" has significance when it is compared to the passage in the myth that describes how the girl "stepped on the mud and began to mix it with her foot." The figure to the left with no head, a phallus and a humped back is gesturing toward the two copulating figures. These two copulating figures, in turn, are connected to the zigzag line symbols by a short wavy line. This connecting line indicates a direct association between the conception (copulating couple) and the figure incorporated into the zigzag symbol. These three symbols in context with each other convey the idea of copulation-fertilization in association with the movement of arms and legs (mixing of mud). The conception from the mud is illustrated further by the line leading from the right foot/zigzag incorporation, up into the figure's body. (La Van Martineau, personal conversation, January, 1988). Chart 3 illustrates symbol incorporation and symbol combinations in an effort to show how these symbols can be "unpacked" and better understood from their component parts.

Within the context of the myth, the symbols together describe the act of the girl mixing the clay for her mother and stamping it with one foot, as described in the story. From the viewpoint of the myth, these symbols together clarify the idea that the pregnancy was caused by something in the mud or water, and not by one of the suitors in the previous panel.

Below the zigzag symbol, to the right, is a large bird. Its feet are touching a crack leading down and to the right. Its breast is large and pointed. The position of the bird is turned away from the other symbols but the tail is still touching them to indicate a relationship of some kind.

The use of animals or birds as metaphors becomes more clear at this point. In the myth, the mother instructs her daughter how to mix the mud and stamp on it with her feet. She then turns away and leaves to get more water. "You keep on doing this for me," she says, and turns away. The mother is represented here by the bird that is walking away from the figure mixing the mud and water. This bird has an unusually large breast, to identify it as the "mother" (La Van Martineau, personal conversation, January, 1988). The feet are touching a crack that leads down and away to the right. This bird is used a second time in Panel 4, drawn with the same enlarged breast to distinguish it from other more ordinary looking birds. This "mother" bird appears in the appropriate context within the myth and Panel 4 later on. [2]

In Panel 2 is an object drawn as two lobes connected by a cross bar that is similar to double-lobed pottery found in the Southwest. Such pottery is shown in Figure 37 from Chaco Canyon, dated around A.D. 1100, Figure 38 from Kayenta dated around A.D. 1203-1273, and Figure 39 from Cochiti, dated to the 1900s. Double-lobed jars are considered highly ceremonial of a metaphorical utility for ritual and ceremony. The metaphor of the double-lobed jar is discussed later.

Pictured on this panel, near the double-lobed jar, is the symbol of a flute player. Notice it does not have a hump back or a phallus. This figure is merely playing a flute and gesturing up toward a couple in copulation. In many pueblo origin myths, it is said that life forms were *sung* into being. The flute player was commissioned by the Creator for music that brings things to life. Here the flute player is playing and gesturing toward the copulating couple, to promote life from the strange conception. He is also in association with the next symbol, the quadruped. It is in a vertical position, to the right of the flute player.

The quadruped belongs to the category of "sign vehicle" discussed previously. Its vertical position indicates "moving upward" or straight up as in "growing up." One horn has been pecked-in with dots that are symbolic of particles of water. This pecking method refers to being "wet" in some contexts, or corn meal in others (Dutton 1963). The other horn is sharp and clear to indicate the opposite of "wet," that of being "dry." The quadruped is moving upward and away from the "wet" horn and on toward the position of the "dry" horn. Within the context of the myth, the sign vehicle illustrates the boy coming to life and "growing up" in a "wet" place and moving toward an adult life in a "dry" place.

That the quadruped is used as a sign vehicle is evident by its unusual position, body shape, and variation in horn shape and texture. Placed here, the quadruped fills in important information about the condition and status of the main character without the necessary cultural contexting that the other images require in order to understand their meaning. A breakdown of this quadruped is shown in Chart 3 of Symbol Incorporations and Combinations.

Figure 37. Double lobed jar from Chaco Canyon circa 1100 A.D., Chaco Culture National Historic Park, NM.

Figure 38. Double lobed jar from Kayenta circa 1200-1273 A.D., private collection.

Figure 39. Double lobed jar from Cochiti circa 1900 A.D. Millicent Rogers Museum, Taos, NM.

54

Water Jar Boy asks his grandfather to take him hunting as shown in the next sequence of events illustrated in Panel 3, Figure 33. Figure 34 is an illustration of Panel 4. Here is found the image of a mountain lion that is identified by his long body and tail, and facial whiskers. The mountain lion is traditionally considered the symbol of a great hunter by both Eastern and Western Pueblo societies. The lion symbol can evoke the whole concept of " going hunting with the power and ability of the great mountain lion." It is a symbol of the supreme hunter, who "has power to attract deer, antelope, and the power to be lucky, i.e. "succeed" (Parsons 1939:335). Eastern Pueblo hunters carry their arrows in a mountain lion skin quiver. They make shrines in the mountains to the north of their villages for the mountain lion spiritual power to assist them in their hunting seasons. They may even "feed" a mountain lion fetish blood from fresh game to encourage the lion to attract more game in the future.

In the myth, Water Jar Boy asks to go hunting with his grandfather, spies a rabbit and rolls along in pursuit. Within the context of the myth, the mountain lion symbol found in Panel 3, is used to represent the boy in the act of "hunting."[3] This idea is supported by the context of the other images in the panel. In the myth, during the hunt, the Water Jar Boy accidentally hits a rock and breaks open. This is illustrated in the panel with the symbol of the water jar breaking open and particles (of water) streaming out of both lobes of the jar. These dotted particles refer to water leaking out the sides (not the top), to indicate the jar was broken.

To the left of the water jar is a very sparsely pecked (dotted) human figure. His legs are positioned to show him still on one knee and rising on the other leg. The figure is textured with peck marks, indicating "wet" and associating him with the substance leaking out of the water jar. Together, these symbols relate the mythic incident of the water jar breaking and the boy emerging. The interpretation of this sequence of events portrayed in the symbols include, "hunting," "pursuing," "double lobed jar," "leaking moisture," "a figure kneeling and covered with moisture." They are in agreement with the events or constituent units found in the myth.

"Animals-as-metaphors" is demonstrated in Panel 2 with the use of the bird symbol representing the girl's mother, and further demonstrated in Panels 3 and 4 with the use of a mountain lion. The exercise of transcending our fixation from the "animal" or "bird" identification, to the "meaning" intended is essential in the reading of a myth or a visual representation of a myth (Campbell 1986).[4]

The mountain lion symbol is carried over to Panel 4, Figure 34, where it is placed next to a coil. A short coil is used in sign language gesture to denote going up or down. A clockwise turn *inward* represents "ascending". A coil turning counter clockwise inward means "descending," as an eagle does when he spirals around to catch the up-drafts (Martineau 1973:19). Extended meanings of the coil can be a "whirl wind," a "spring," or a "snake." Snakes and springs are in most cases, synonymous. In pueblo mythology, a snake always lives in a spring. The long coils are referred to as "spirals" which usually represent a great distance in travel or in time. It may often refer to a journey of people "to a Center Place."[5] The coil, in this panel, has been pecked with many dots, and the reference to "water" has thereby been added. A symbol breakdown of this image is found in Chart 3, from Panel 4.

In the context of the myth, the combination of "wet" and "descend down" refers to descending into water or a spring. The myth recounts how the boy goes to the spring "in search of" or "hunting" his father. Water Jar Boy insists on knowing who his real father is and his strong intent is again represented by the mountain lion, the hunter and seeker, positioned near the spring.

In the myth, the father meets the boy at the spring and together they travel down into the spring. There he is greeted by his sisters and aunts. The "Center Place" inside the spring is represented by the circle with a line through it, indicating "passed through the center." The birds, as with the mountain lion, are carried over from previous panels to represent the relatives of the boy, who in the myth meets his sisters and aunts inside the spring. The myth states that the boy's mother dies but rejoins him back inside the spring. She is identified in this panel as the bird with a large breast that symbolizes "mother." She is located near the top of the spring. The boy's father is identified as Avanyu, the water serpent, who lives inside the spring, and also may be represented by the coil.

Chart 4 is presented as an analysis of the etic and emic perspective used in the interpretation presented. First, the panel is broken down into its component parts and each image is analyzed from an etic (outside) perspective. Symbol description, symbol combinations, sign language and body posture, spatial syntax and spatial positioning are categories used to analyze the petroglyph images. Second, the myth is broken down into constituent units that make up the structure of the myth. This comprises the emic (inside) contextual information. The final category is the panel interpretation within the mythic context. Here the integration of both the emic and etic perspective allow for a more holistic interpretation.

CONCLUSION

The interpretation of this petroglyph depends upon the understanding of metaphors that are used in myth by the pueblo. The above discussion draws the reader's understanding away from an etic perception of representational objects or animals and leads it toward the emic metaphorical interpretation that is found within the myth itself.

An interpretation of the myth "Water Jar Boy" has been put forth by Joseph Campbell in his book *The Hero with a Thousand Faces*. Though he never knew of a possible visual representation of this myth, these images support Campbell's interpretations. He writes of Water Jar Boy:

> The child of destiny has to face a long period of obscurity. This is a time of extreme danger, impediment or disgrace. He is thrown inward to his own depths or outward to the unknown; either way, what he touches is a darkness unexplored...after a long period of obscurity his true character is revealed. This event may precipitate a considerable crisis; for it amounts to an emergence of powers hitherto excluded from human life. Earlier patterns break to fragments or dissolve..the creative value of the new factor comes to view...the adventure of the second is the going to the father - the father is the invisible unknown.....Where the goal of the hero's effort is the discovery of the unknown father, the basic symbolism remains that of the tests and the self-revealing way...The hero blessed by the father returns to represent the father among men...Since he is now centered in the source, he makes visible the repose and harmony of the central place. He is a reflection of the World Axis from which the concentric circles spread - the World Mountain, the World Tree - he is the perfect microcosmic mirror of the macrocosm. To see him is to perceive the meaning of existence. From his presence boons go out; his word is the wind of life.
>
> Campbell 1949:326-347

The double-lobed jar represents the duality of the earthly world in which the boy was born and the watery dark abyss in which the boy grew up. That metaphor is translated to the image of the double-lobed jar to incorporate the concept of the dualism that exists in every aspect of pueblo life. It is found in their clan systems and moieties, in the cosmos, the creation myths and in their world views. Ortiz (1972:144) emphasizes this concept of duality:

> The grand dualities of the cosmos also serve to unify space and time and other, lesser dualities that reverberate through Pueblo life....The basic level of dualities that in nature, winter and summer, provide the fundamental principle of organization for the ritual calendar...Other dualities cut across all of existence, from the hot and the cold to the raw and the cooked and the ripe and the unripe, sometimes all at once.

Others have also written on the concept of duality in pueblo world views. Levi-Strauss writes that the actions of the unconscious mind expresses itself through social forms. "A moiety system ...makes a visible representation of the mind's natural proclivity to divide and subdivide." (Strauss in Douglas 1982:165)   It is this dualistic physical world that the boy has to transcend in order to enter into the spirit world. The mountain lion image in the panel is a symbol for "hunting," "seeking" or "pursuing with great intent," whether for rabbits or the spiritual quest to find his father. The theme occurs over and over in pueblo mythology, when the son of a virgin birth asks the question: "Who is my father?" and sets forth "seeking" to find him, whether he be the sun, the wind or the water. The hero has to overcome tremendous obstacles using sheer determination and intuitive power. The mountain lion is a metaphor for such profound intent and seeking out these metaphysical objectives. Joseph Campbell (1986:56) writes that, "The distinguishing function of a properly read mythology is to release the mind from its naive fixation...in material things as things-in-themselves. Hence the figurations of myth are metaphorical in two senses simultaneously, as both psychological, and at the same time metaphysical." In this case, the double-lobed jar is the dualities on the psychological plane, from which the boy has to break free in order to find the source of his spiritual being.

The petroglyph image of the coil spiraling inward to a center point and circle is consistent with the pueblo's use of the symbol of the middle or center of the cosmos represented by a "Sipapu," an Earth navel, or emergence place. This sacred space may be visually represented by a small circle in the center of a sand painting, a ring of rocks in the village plaza or a hole in the floor of a kiva.   Ortiz (1972:142) states, "The elaboration of the notion of the center has the further implication that the dominant spatial orientation, as well as that of motion, is centripetal or inward. That is to say, all things are defined and represented by reference to a center."

The coil is a symbol combination of both a trail and water. It is multireferential, representing the dwelling place of the water snake, the pathway to the underworld and the source of life-giving water. On another level, it represents the spiritual world, the dwelling place of the unconscious, the source of the life-giving spirit, the home of "The Father," and the home to which one returns after death. Jane Young (1988:105-106) writes about multireferential symbols in the pueblo world and particularly for the Zuni: "They are standing for both themselves and something else at the same time, yet all of the meanings are bound together, so that the Zuni say, *They are all the same thing. "*

It is highly probable that this petroglyph represents the Water Jar Boy myth of pueblo oral tradition, based on the above description and correspondence between the drawings and the myth. Investigations made by Martineau (1973), Dutton (1963), Parsons (1939), Cushing (1979), Young (1985), Schaafsma (1989) and others who have studied traditional visual art of the Pueblo Indians conclude that in Indian pictography there was little concern with realistic representations of actual animals or people. Nancy Olsen (1989:423) summarizes:

> When the meanings are restored to form and context, documented evidence of social categories emerges such that animals, birds, reptiles, and amphibians are used exclusively to refer to man-made situations; such as clan symbols, as representatives of power for curing, as assistants to spirits and kachinas, and as messengers for the People. In the emic view,

animals have power to travel between men and spirits/kachinas to mediate between them. The natural abilities of an animal or bird are interwoven with their powers in myth and histories.

What has been suggested with myth also holds true with the visual depictions of myths. The stylistic or simplified gesture figures are metaphors used to transmit the meaning or essence of character imbued in these beings. Animals used as metaphors have more to do with a metaphysical and psychological meaning. They enable the viewer to transcend aspects of the physical realm to one of greater complexity and spiritual meaning within the context of pueblo cosmology and world view.

ENDNOTES

1. Parsons designates the Water Jar Boy myth as Tewa in origin. It also is recorded at Hano, a Tewa village at Hopi. The Southern Tewa or "Tano" people who fled to Hopi in 1696, were originally from the Galisteo Basin of the Rio Grande Valley. During the Indian Revolt of 1680, the Keresan pueblos of San Marcos and La Cienega joined the Tanos in the attack on Santa Fe. The years following were of tremendous struggle and relocation. Those Southern Tewa who did not go to Hopi, joined neighboring pueblos, both Tewa and Keresan. Most of the evidence determining the linguistic affiliation of La Cienega suggests an influence of both Tano (Southern Tewa) and Keresan. It therefore is not a complete mystery how the appearance of Tewa mythology, associated with a petroglyph, could be found alongside a Keresan myth-related petroglyph in the same site. Petroglyph dating is still relatively impossible, but someday a way may be found to determine an accurate date for the rendering of this panel and better qualify its cultural origin.

2. The bird is used at Cochiti to represent the "mother of the people." This image is used in more specific ways, such as the "bird with the one cross-foot," and the association with the "Corn Mother" is implied (personal conversation with Joe Herrera, September, 1989).

3. As the Zuni shaman (Big Firebrand Society) drops his pulverized roots into the medicine bowl, he prays:

> Yonder in the north
> You who are my father,
> Mountain lion,
> You are life-giving society chief;
> Bring your medicine
> You will make your road come hither.
> Where lies my white shell bowl,
> Watch over my spring.
> When you sit down quietly,
> *We shall be one person.*
> (Parsons, 1939:416)

4. Joseph Campbell, (1986:56) *The Inner Reaches of Outer Space*, writes, " The distinguishing function of a properly read mythology is to release the mind from its naive fixation...on material things as things-in-themselves. Hence the figurations of myth (and in symbolic art) are metaphorical in two senses simultaneously, as both psychological, and at the same time metaphysical."

5. Jane Young (1985:136) writes: " The spiral could be described as referring to this event from two different perspectives. The central point of the spiral is itself a condensed symbol, but so is the rest of the figure; years of travel and hardship are encoded in the inward-turning coils. It is of interest that the Zunis, with whom I worked perceived a figure that could be seen as "opening out" as "turning inward" instead. They described the journey in search of the Center as motion through time directed inward, often following the coils of the spiral in toward the center point with their fingertips. This perspective is quite consistent with the inner-or-center-directed ethos of the Zuni people."

In Cochiti, Lange (1959:94) refers to the men planting their fields, by beginning at the edge of the field and working in a spiral, counter clockwise towards the center where they finished.

Water Jar Boy Panel 1 at la Cienega.

Water Jar Boy Panel 2 at la Cienega.

PLATE 3

Panel 3 of the Water Jar Boy petroglyph.

Panel 4 of the Water Jar Boy petroglyph.

PLATE 4

Petroglyph Panel of Uretsete and Naotsete Genesis Myth at La Cienega.

PLATE 5

Close up on the lower panel depicting the two sisters

PLATE 6

4
URETSETE AND NAOTSETE ORIGIN MYTH

In the beginning Tsechenako, Thought Woman, finished everything, thoughts,and the names of all things. She finished also all the languages. And then our mothers, Uretsete and Naotsete said they would make names and they would make thoughts. Thus they said, Thus they did..

_____ Keresan Pueblo saying, (Purley 1974:29)

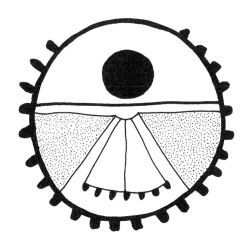

The origin myth of Uretsete and Naotsete has been recorded by several ethnographers during the past century. It is fundamental to the religious beliefs of the Keresan pueblos located along the Rio Grande, including, Cochiti, Santo Domingo, San Felipe, Santa Anna, Acoma, Zia, and Laguna. The linguistic areas are shown in Figure 3 in Chapter 1.

The first written record of this myth is found in the notes recorded by Father Noel Dumarest, a French priest who was assigned to Peña Blanca in 1894 and served the surrounding pueblo villages of Santo Domingo, Cochiti and San Felipe. He was very close to the people and sought to record and preserve their native culture. In 1900 he contracted malaria and died, but Dumarest's manuscripts were later translated into English by Elsie Clews Parsons and published as his *Notes on Cochiti, New Mexico* in 1919.

Versions of this myth are retold at Zia Pueblo (Stevenson 1894), San Felipe and Acoma (White 1932; Stirling 1942) and Laguna (Gunn 1917; Boas and Parsons 1928). Since Cochiti Pueblo is closest in proximity to the petroglyph site and in cultural association, the names and spelling as Dumarest recorded them will be used as the model for comparison purposes. Important elements are in boldface type in the story for the benefit of the reader as a reference guide to the discussion that follows. Dumarest recorded the following:

ORIGIN MYTH OF URETSETE AND NAOTSETE

Uretsete was the mother of the Indians, and **Naotsete,** the elder sister, was the **mother of the Whites and Navajos.** They both wanted to go to the south to people the country there. Naotsete challenged her younger sister to a contest of powers to determine which should have the privilege.

The elder sister said one day to the younger sister who lived somewhere in the north in a house with four rooms, "Come, I have need of you." She showed her a **road of corn meal** that led from the west to a room in the east. On this road were the **tracks of a bird.**

Naotsete said to Uretsete, "Look at these tracks. Can you tell me to what creature they belong?"

Uretsete was wise. She did not speak at once. She said sadly, "These tracks go from west to east."

Naotsete said quickly, "What creature do they belong to? Call it by name."

The younger sister said, **"Turkey Man,** come out from your hiding place."

The creature was indeed a turkey. He came out. He sat down next to Uretsete and said to her, "Mother, here I am." And he leaned his head against her cheek as if to caress her.

Naotsete got irritated and said, "You are only a witch. I am quite right in always calling you this."

A little later Uretsete called her sister and said to her, "I need you here. Look at these tracks. Can you tell me the direction they go in?"

The tracks of the time before had this form (the narrator marked ⟨) but the direction of the tracks Uretsete showed to Naotsete were much more difficult to tell. They had this form ⟩⟨ .

Meanwhile Naotsete considered them casually and, laughing, said to her sister, "These tracks certainly go to the east. How could you have shut up this creature in the west in a room filled with a refuse heap of ashes and filth?" "It is certainly a crow. There are no other creatures which make such tracks."

"Crow Man," said she, "turn to the east, come out."

A silence followed. Naotsete looked cross. She began to see her mistake. Then Uretsete turned to the east and said, "Chaparral-cock come out!"

Then the **Chaparral Cock** came out from the room on the east and approached Uretsete in a friendly way to join the turkey in caring for her. Angered, Naotsete again called her sister a witch and withdrew sadly.

Another day she called her sister and said to her, "Uretsete, my sister, look at these tracks on the road of meal. Whose are they?"

Uretsete began to weep, for she was afraid of being defeated. Her sister scolded her saying Uretsete was not a witch. She heard the voice of Kopershtaia who encouraged her and promised her success.

Then she said, "This track is that of a serpent."

"But of what serpent?"

"Of a rattlesnake."

"You see I am right in calling you a witch...And in what direction does he go?"

"To the northeast."

Then Uretsete turned to the northeast and said. **"Serpent Man**, come out." And the serpent came out, saying, "My mother, here I am." And Uretsete took some **cornmeal and put it on the head of the serpent** who took it into his mouth with his tongue, and approached Uretsete with affection.

Naotsete said to the serpent, "You may go with your mother to hell. I do not want you."

And the serpent answered, "Yes, I want to stay with my mother." A final trial was made. Uretsete called her sister and showed her tracks like those of the crow. She said to her elder sister, "Whose tracks are these, my sister?"

Naotsete got angry and said to her, "Witch, why do you always make it hard for me?"

"My sister, I did not challenge you. It was you who obliged me to take part in the struggle."

Then Naotsete examined the tracks of the bird and said, "These are tracks of a crow coming from the south." And turning to the north she said, **"Crow Man,** come out." She received no response.

Then Uretsete, turning to the south, said, "Tehana Man , come out." And he came out and lined up on the side of Uretsete.

Naotsete was so angry she wanted to strike her sister and she seized her by the hair.

But Uretsete said to her, "No, my sister, I do not want to harm you, nor have you harm me. You were the first to challenge, but listen, we are going to meet a final test and, if you agree, after a fast of four days, we will stand on the same line, facing the east. You are bigger than I, you have the advantage."

Naotsete agreed.

Then the two sisters gave notice to their fathers, mothers, brothers and children. The people of the place divided into two sides; one for Naotsete the other for Uretsete. Both sides made **arrows** during the four days the sisters fasted, because the sides too, were to fight against each other after the test of the sisters.

At the end of four days the sisters took a stand side by side on **top of a little hill.** On top of her head each had an upright eagle **feather.** Naotsete, who stood to the north was a head taller than her sister, and chance appeared to be in her favor. Behind the sisters were the captains and the sub-captains charged with watching. Then came further back the two groups.

Then Spider Man sent Magpie (Shrouakaia) or (Hakiaia) to the east. **Magpie spread a wing** over the northern part of the sun and covered it, particularly the top of it. Thus when the first rays reached the two sisters they **fell first on the top of the feather** worn by Uretsete, and when they fell on the feather of Naotsete they were already lighting up the shoulders of Uretsete.

Uretsete said, "Only look, my sister. **I have won."** Naotsete did not answer and turned her head so as not to see.

After several moments of silence, Uretsete took her sister by the arms and made her look. Naotsete, conquered, said, "Yes, you kill me."

The younger sister seized her body, and the captains helped to **tie** her and throw her down. Naotsete said, "Yes, kill me and go to the south, since you have beaten me, but let me say one thing before I die." And she said, "Know this, the Earth must be thickly peopled, and our sons will be just like ourselves."

Then Uretsete cut open her chest between the ribs, tore out her **heart, split it through the middle** and spread open each half. From the **north side came out a squirrel** and from the **south side a white dove.** Uretsete then went into Sipapu, separating from her children. Before they left, she said to them, "My children, you must leave. I remain. Keep from quarreling. Do not follow the example of my elder sister. If you do not follow my advice, you will regret it. However, if you get into trouble, send for me and I will help you."

During the journey to the south disputes began, bad words and rows of all sorts divided the people. Their punishment was a great epidemic which decimated them. Then they said, "Let us send **Coyote** to Uretsete, that he may fetch from our mother a remedy for our ills." Coyote said, " I go very willingly."

He ran hard. On arriving, he recounted to Uretsete the misfortunes of the people. She began to laugh and said, "What has happened? They have not followed my advice and have behaved themselves badly?"

Coyote said, "I do not know."

Uretsete said to him, "Go to the people and take them these packages of meal and of tobacco, and tell them to send me two from among themselves."

Two men arrived. During the journey of Coyote and of the men, Uretsete had reflected upon a means of remedying the ills of her sons. She had **planned an 'Iariko.'** She wound thongs of deer hide about an ear of corn and placed at its top **feathers** of a turkey, which at her order had shaken out its feathers for her.

But finding that her work was not perfect, she had called Spider, saying to him, "I have wished to make for my people something endowed with the same power as myself, and to give it to them. I know that you are thoughtful. How does my work seem to you?"

Spider said, "It is good, but at the top put some parrot feathers, and at the neck some eagle-down, and all will be well."

Uretsete did this, and thus was created the Iariko, which she gave to the two men sent by the emigrants. She said to the two, after having initiated them into the mysteries of the Chaiani, "This has the same power as I. Take it to my people, that the sick may recover health."

These two men, made Chaiani or medicine-men, returned to the people with the order to confer on others the same power that they themselves had received. Then they set themselves to curing people, and cures took place in great number.

Dumarest 1919: 212-216 reprinted with permission from the American Anthropological Association, Memoirs, 6.

Figure 40.   Ink drawing of entire panel of Uretsete and Naotsete

IDENTIFICATION OF THE SYMBOLS

The next panel discussed in association with this myth is found further along the cliff face above La Cienega. Uretsete and Naotsete are identified in the panel shown in Figure 40, by their maiden hair whorls, typical of pueblo maidens in prehistoric times. The arm and leg positions of these two figures indicate action, perhaps of running or wrestling. The same body shape indicates they are sisters or "of the same kind of body." Naotsete is identified as the taller of the two, the eldest, as is stated in the myth. Uretsete is smaller, and younger, but is the smarter of the two. An illustration of this panel is shown in Plate 5.

In the myth, a conflict between the two sisters arises over who shall have the privilege of peopling the country to the south. In the panel, this *conflict* is represented by the arrowhead touching the head of the first bird on the left. Arrow points represent "conflict" and in this panel, they are associated with the bird's head by touching it. The "head" refers to a name or identity. The first bird has one cross-foot and is identified as Uretsete's counterpart symbol. She is being challenged by Naotsete. Her symbol is repeated in each episode hereafter. Figure 41 shows this section of the panel.

Naotsete challenges Uretsete to name the different bird tracks running through a trail of corn meal as the birds cross from east to west or west to east. Rock incorporation has been utilized to designate the corn meal trail. The rock has a dull vertical edge, that runs down the center of the panel. The birds are placed so their feet are touching this edge which represents the "corn meal trail." The first bird has only one foot, as explained above, as the bird with the one cross-foot. This bird, represents Uretsete and the conflict (arrow) with Naotsete in general.

The second bird to the right in this conflict, also has his head touching an arrow point but his **two** feet are touching the ridge used to represent the cornmeal trail. This is likely to represent Turkey Man. He allies with Uretsete, which further irritates Naotsete.

Naotsete guesses the identity of the third bird in the conflict as Crow Man, but this is wrong. Uretsete corrects her and calls forth Chaparral Cock Man. In the myth, Naotsete is confused by the bird's track and the direction in which it was traveling. The third bird in this panel has an arrow point touching its foot and its other foot is touching the ridge or corn meal trail. This symbol arrangement denotes a conflict over the foot of the bird symbolizing "track" or "direction." As we have learned earlier, Chaparral Cock, or roadrunner, is known for his confusing track.

The bird in Figure 42 appears in each panel and is associated with Uretsete as a specific aspect of her abilities called for throughout the story. Notice that this bird with one cross-foot is standing at the top of the main panel. Uretsete is known to provide rain for her people and is depicted as a rain bird in some cases. Dumarest (1919:173) states that when Uretsete wants it to rain she sends a messenger to the *Shiwanna* to distribute the rain.[1]

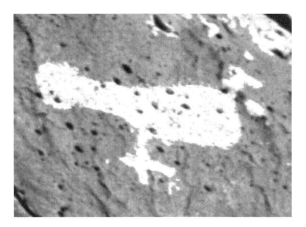

Figure 41. (left) Detail of the left section of the panel of Urestete and Naotsete.

Figure 42. (right) Close up of the bird with one cross-foot.

Uretsete has been identified as a bird woman, with wings, a tail and one leg with talons, and the head of a woman in an altar painting for the Fire Society altar of Acoma as shown in Figure 43.

The rim is blue, representing the sky, the sun is red, and the moon is yellow. The Milky Way is pale gray. Uretsete's face and body have yellow spots that represent the Earth. The arrowhead on her breast is red and represents the center of the earth and the world.

Other bird woman portraits e.g. Figure 44, appear in the kiva murals at Pottery Mound that may be of Keresan influence.

Figure 43. A sand painting from Acoma depicting the Uretsete as a bird woman. (After Stirling, 1942)

Figure 44. Kiva mural painting from Pottery Mound depicting a bird woman. (After Hibben, 1975)

To the far left is the symbol of the Serpent Man. The wavy line represents the trail of Serpent Man as he crawls through the cornmeal from northeast to south. As discussed before, the dotted pecking technique refers to "particles of something." In context with the myth, these particles represent cornmeal. The head of the serpent is diamond shaped, which is similar to the serpents depicted in Kiva murals. Serpent Man's head is crossed by the line of cornmeal that Uretsete placed upon his head as stated in the myth. Figure 45 is a close-up of Serpent Man crawling through the corn meal trail.

Figure 45.   Close up of panel depicting the snake and the corn meal trail.

Figure 46 is a painting of a snake in the kiva mural art of the Pottery Mound site. The basic head shape is the same as in the petroglyph.

Figure 46.   Image of a snake from Pottery Mound. (After Hibben, 1975)

The bird to the right of the Serpent Man is Crow Man, whom Naotsete guessed correctly. Crow Man did not respond to Naotsete's call but came out only for Uretsete, from the south along the corn meal trail to the north. There is no arrow over his head, perhaps because Naotsete did not guess his name wrong. The three birds, Uretsete (as a bird) and snake are identified here.

Uretsete   Turkey Man   Chaparral Cock   Serpent Man   Crow Man

Uretsete and Naotsete prepare for the final test. The two sisters fasted for four days. During this time the people made arrows preparing for a final battle. In the panel there is a line of arrow points representing "conflict," with one arrow touching the bare foot, which in many cases represents "battle" as expressed in the common phrase "barefoot or stripped for battle." Figure 47 is a close-up of this section of the panel.

Figure 47.   Close up of arrows and bare foot in the panel.

The two sisters agree to go to the top of a hill at dawn and face the east. Footprints are shown going up the side of the panel toward the "testing ground." In the myth, each sister wears a feather on top of her head. Both women face the rising sun to determine whom the rays shall strike first. "Naotsete, who stood to the north, was a head taller than her sister, and chance appeared to be in her favor." Spider sends Magpie to the east and he spreads a wing over the northern part of the sun, covering the top of it. "Thus when the first rays reached the two sisters they fell first on the top of the feather worn by Uretsete and when they fell on the feather of Naotsete they were already lighting up the shoulders of Uretsete." Following the foot prints to the top section of the panel are the symbols depicting a striated magpie wing and a dotted trail of sunlight leading to the lower feather tip. Figure 48 shows a close-up of this section.

Figure 48.   Close up of the magpie wing
and trail of sunlight down
to the lower feather tip in
the panel.

The panel depicts this whole sequence of events. The half-circle symbol that is striated black and white represents the wing of the magpie. A magpie's wing is black outside with white feathers inside. When opened, light will pass through the white portions of the wing. See Figure 49.

Figure 49.
Photograph of an
outstretched magpie
wing.

Figure 50 is a wooden ritual object found in a room in Chetro Ketl.[2]   The wooden bird has the striated wing outstretched, similar to image drawn in the panel. There is strong evidence that the Keresan culture flourished in Chaco Canyon, and further research of the petroglyphs from Chaco and their relationship to Keresan myths is under way.

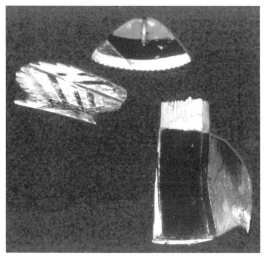

Figure 50.   On right, reconstructed wooden ritual bird from Chaco Canyon with the striated wing similar to the wing depicted in the petroglyph panel. On left, actual wooden artifacts from which bird was reconstructed. Courtesy National Park Service.

In the panel, the dots coming up out of the top of the "wing" and down the side and around to the two "feather tips" indicate a trail of sunlight coming down from the wing of the magpie to the lower feather tip. The feather tips are distinguished by their rounded ends. Arrow tips are sharp and distinct. Examples of both are found in kiva murals and their separate identities in some instances have been confused by others.[3]

In Stevenson's version (1894:34) of the myth, more details are given of the next event:

> The two women stood still while the men fought. The women remained on the mountain's top, but the men *descended* into a grassy park to fight. After a time the younger sister [Uretsete] ran [down] to the park and cried 'This is enough; fight no more.' She then returned to the mountain and said to her sister, 'Let us *descend* to the park and fight.' And they fought like women - not with arrows - but wrestled.

In the petroglyph, Uretsete and Naotsete both have their arms and legs in active positions. This indicates they were engaged in running and fighting. The figure to the left is a symbol combination of a person with turkey-track hands. As we have learned previously, the turkey tracks show direction. This symbol combination refers to "descending" as Uretsete and Naotsete are said to have done before they fought. Figure 51 is a close-up of the symbol combination of a man with turkey-track hands directing Uretsete and Naotsete downward. A symbol breakdown of this symbol is found in Chart 4.

Figure 51. Figure in the upper left area of the panel is a sign vehicle that incorporates the human arm gesture and turkey track hands indicating a downward movement.

The outcome of the battle between the two sisters is symbolized by the two pairs of bare feet. The lower pair are larger and connected by a line that refers to Naotsete, who was held down and tied by the War Captains. The feet above are smaller and represent Uretsete. Their positioning symbolizes "dominance" or the resulting outcome, referring to Uretsete overcoming Naotsete in the battle. Figure 52 is an illustration of both pairs of feet.

Figure 52. Close up on the two pairs of feet in the panel. The upper pair is smaller, depicting Uretsete. The lower pair is larger, depicting Naotsete. The lower pair is connected by a line indicating Naotsete was tied up.

In the myth, Uretsete cuts open her sister's chest, takes out her heart, and splits it in half. From the north side came a squirrel and from the south side came a dove.

The symbol for this event is the incorporation of a dove and a squirrel as shown in a close-up in Figure 53.

Figure 53.   Close up on the symbol combination of a dove (wing) and packrat (body).

The dove is identified by its feet (bird feet) and its wing (dove wing). The head is touching the heart position of the second figure, indicating a relationship to the heart. The second figure has a large round pack and a small rodent-like head, depicting a woodrat, sometimes called a packrat. It must be noted that the squirrel and rat are one in the same woodrat, which thrives on cactus.[4] Packrats store food for future need in their dens and may be analogous to humans that travel with their necessities in a backpack. The hand of this figure is holding its penis, a symbol for procreation. The legs of the figure are separated, a body gesture indicating "going in opposite directions" or splitting apart. The symbols collectively represent the splitting of the heart (dove touching the heart position), into a dove (dove wing and foot), and a woodrat (rodent head and body). The symbol of procreation is in reference to the struggle between the two sisters that caused the fight. Before she dies, Naotsete gives warning that "all our sons will be just like ourselves." This statement has to do again with procreation, the right to people the land to the south, with the resulting people having attributes of both sisters. Stevenson's version (1889:34) elaborates on this scene:

73

She held the heart in her hand and cried: "Listen, men and youths! This woman was my sister, but she compelled us to fight; it was she who taught you to fight. The few of her people who escaped are in the mountains and they are the people of the rats". She cut the heart into pieces and threw it upon the ground, saying, "Her heart will become rats, for it was very bad," and immediately rats could be seen running in all directions. She found the center of the heart full of cactus, and she said, "The rats for evermore will live with the cacti;" and to this day the rats thus live (referring to the Neotoma [the woodrat]). She then told her people to return to their homes.

It is noted by Parsons that the outcome of this myth is "the reason why Pueblo people, the children of Uretsete were always victorious against the Navajo, the children of Naotsete. Naotsete had said, `Just as the squirrel from my heart will find safety under the cliffs and in holes, so my children will seek refuge in flight and in dens among the rocks...' that is why Navajos still save themselves among the rocks" (footnote by Parsons in Dumarest 1919:215).

Uretsete then went to the Sipapu, which is beneath the ground. She is represented again here by the bird with one cross-foot. She is pictured near the center of the panel in Figure 54.

Figure 54.   Close up on a portion of the panel depicting the bird with one cross-foot that represents Uretsete as she descends down the crack into the underworld.

Her one cross-foot is touching a large crack in the rock running downward, indicating a trail leading "down to the underworld." The bird figure is repeated a second time, lower down, as a very faint bird, which indicates "disappearing into the underworld" (Martineau, 1989).

In the myth, the people eventually fall into ill ways. Coyote is sent by the people to ask Uretsete for help. He is shown in the far right corner, drawn as a simple dog-like animal. His mouth is touching the crack that leads to the underworld to which Uretsete descended. His mouth is open and touching the crack to indicate that he is talking to her.

Uretsete responds to Coyote's request by making an *Iariko*, or corn fetish, with which to help her people. She takes a perfect ear of corn, shown by the symbol of an ear of corn, and attaches feathers to it that she gathers from Turkey, who gives them to her at her request. This transaction is portrayed in Figure 55.

Figure 55. Close up on a portion of the panel that depicts the birds giving feathers to make the Iariko.

The taking of feathers from a live bird for medicinal and ceremonial fetishes is a common practice in the Southwest (Parsons in Dumarest 1919:213). The first bird in this group of symbols is shown with a line drawn to its foot and attached to a feather tip. The second bird is touching the feather with its beak. Together, the symbols indicate the bird was asked (line to mouth) and the bird gave (line to foot) feathers (feather symbol at other end of line) to Uretsete willingly. The next symbol down is the perfect ear of corn with feathers being attached, thus creating the Iariko. The Iariko is further explained in detail in a separate panel further along the cliff face, and discussed in Chapter 6.

Chart 5 is an analysis from the etic and emic perspective. The etic view utilizes the categories of symbol description, symbol combinations, sign language body posture, spatial syntax and spatial positioning. The emic view is presented in terms of the mythic constituent units. The final category is an integration of both etic and emic analysis to present a panel interpretation.

CONCLUSION

In Indian cultures generally, sacred myths are supported by their reenactments in ceremonies and representation in official ceremonial offices. Anthony Purley (1974:32) suggests:

> Uretsete and Naotsete are specifically charged with the welfare of the earth and its inhabitants, which includes their assistance as well as the sharing of their powers with mankind and all living things, coexistence between the deities, mankind and all living things is spelled out. Within that coexistence all living things have a function.

Uretsete and Naotsete are the prototype for the social structure of the Keresan culture. It is made up of three parts; the center, the inside, and the outside. Within the center, Uretsete resides, in the Earth as Earth Mother, Mother to all the people. From her came the instructions in curing and religion that are entrusted to the Town Priest. He is the inside chief, in charge of the Corn Mother fetish, the Iariko. The Outside Chiefs are the Country Priest and War Chiefs who must answer to and also get their instructions from the Town Chief. The Outside Chiefs, are the warriors and the hunters, concerned with external activities. The Governor of the Pueblo is an Outside Chief who is the one to deal with aliens and the outside populace. It is in this "outside" realm that Naotsete's people dwell: the Navajos, whites, and aliens.

This structure can be seen in the layout of Keresan pueblos. At the center is the *Hotcanista*, the office of the Town Priest where he can fast and pray and where ceremonial paraphernalia are stored (White 1962:49). To the east is a kiva that is "inside" because it is used by the *cacique* and others for curing and public rituals on behalf of the town. To the west is a kiva that is "outside" because it is associated with hunting and warfare.

Animals are also associated with spatial aspects. At the center of the Keresan cosmic world are the spiritual representatives; the bird that is associated with spirit and Uretsete. To the inside realm belong healing and curing animals such as Bear, who is known for his assistance in curing. The inside realm is the occupational position of the Town Priest whose duties are to practice the curing traditions taught by Uretsete.

The outside realm belongs to game animals and hunting activities. This is the occupational position of the Outside Chief and it is Woodrat who is the bringer of luck to animal hunters. [5]

The symbolic and metaphoric importance of Woodrat becomes clearer in the following pages. Its depiction in a panel further down the canyon is discussed in Chapter 5.

END NOTES

1. For the Pueblo there are three rain birds, the dove, the hummingbird, and the swallow. All three have different qualities that make them special at finding water. The dove is known for its ability to carry the message to the Cloud People to bring rain. Uretsete was often portrayed with the dove, because she herself was asked by the people to bring rain. Her messenger was Dove (Tyler 1979).

2. I came across this example, years after I had already published this symbol as a representation of a magpie wing.

3. Hibben (1975: 130-131, Figures 101 and 102), gives illustrations of arrow tips and feather tips. The difference is evident to the reader. Illustration after Hibben.

4. The *Neotoma cinerea* are defined by Harrington (1914:21) as the bushy-tailed woodrat commonly called a pack rat. The rats or squirrels referred to in the myth are the same "bushy tailed wood rats," that live among the rocks, and pull cactus sprigs around their nests to eat and to protect themselves.

5. Miller (unpublished manuscript 1990:34) states : "In mythology, Cougar is the leader of the animals, functioning as the Social Ego. He won this status by defeating Bear (Benedict 1931:142). Thus, Bear is the inside member, probably joined by other Animal Doctors. On the outside are the Animal Hunters, along with Woodrat as a synecdoche for all wild animal food."

Petroglyph of the woodrat found below the cliff in the canyon floor along the Santa Fe River.

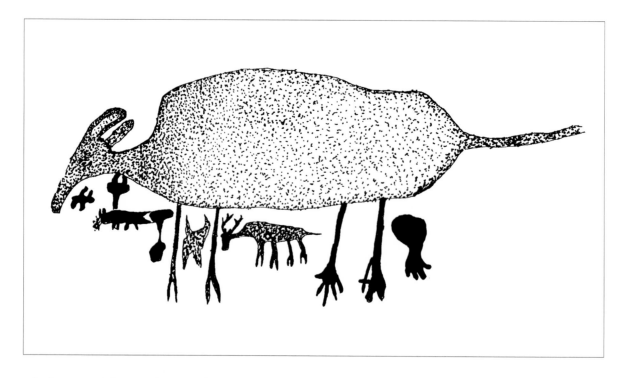

Ink drawing of the woodrat panel

PLATE 7

Petroglyph of the Iariko, Spider Woman, Uretsete and the Bird with one cross-foot.

PLATE 8

Photograph of a painting of an Iariko by Stevenson 1889-90.

PLATE 9

5
RELATED PANELS

The woodrats lived in the mountains.
There were a mother and father and lots of children.
He sang for the children to dance,
I, i, i,Cactus, Cactus
It's useful to us (for a nest)
It's useful to us!
Ha a yot si!
The little woodrats jumped and jumped and rolled over
on the ground. He said,
I'm singing for you,
Try your best!
Try your best!
So we can kill a deer.
They tried hard and their father sang the song.

_____ Cochiti Pueblo Song

Naotsete is the mother of the Navajo and all other aliens. The reader recalls how part of her heart turned into rats that ran among the rocks. The woodrat is a metaphor that is associated with her. As a metaphor, the woodrat has pertinent aspects, such as providing food for her young and shelter among the rocks. This petroglyph panel is located in the bottom of Santa Fe Canyon, adjacent to La Cienega. It is shown in Plate 7.

The larger animal resembles a rat with ears, a large body and long tail. It has hind feet of a rodent, but front feet that are cloven. It stands over smaller animals and animal tracks. This positioning of symbols, a large figure standing over smaller ones, represents a "mother/child" relationship. She is "protecting" smaller ones under her. The smaller figure is a miniature of the larger one. It is different in that it has antlers like a deer. The meaning implied here is "game" animal. The other symbols are animal tracks. They both represent the game or food the mother woodrat provides for her children. This panel simply tells of attributes the Keres have assigned to the woodrat as a metaphor, as a protector of her children (people) and provider of food (game) even in the most severe conditions. Plate 7 also shows a more detailed illustration of the symbols in this panel.

The woodrat is two animals in one, as indicated by its feet. It is two symbols, representing mother/protector of game animals in one sense and Naotsete, mother of Navajos, in the other sense.

In San Felipe and Santo Domingo, the woodrat is called *Ck'a'wac* and is known as the mother of their old time enemy, the Navajo, because it makes a nest of shredded cedar bark for its young, just as a Navajo makes a nest for her baby.[1]   Naotsete said, "Just as the squirrel from my heart will find safety under the cliffs and in holes, so my children will seek refuge in flight and in dens" (Parsons in Dumarest, 1919:213).

From Cochiti there is agreement that this panel depicts the "Mother of the Navajo," who, like the woodrat, protects her children and provides for them. She is thought to bring luck in finding animal tracks and game.

In the past, the men of Laguna, while on a weekly roundup for horses, would catch the wood rats and string them around their horses' necks, in rabbit hunt fashion; the first women to come upon the returning horsemen got the rats (Parsons 1939:110).

Stevenson (1894:26) writes:

"Upon discovering the approach of the herdsmen and horses, many of the women and children, too impatient to await the gathering of them in the corral, hasten to the valley to join the cavalcade and upon reaching the party they at once scramble for the wood rats (Neotoma) that hang from the necks of the horses and colts....The rats are suspended by a yucca ribbon tied around the necks of the animals. ..The rats are skinned and cooked in grease and eaten as a great delicacy."

Figure 56.   Petroglyph panel of Uretsete and Naotsete wrestling, located below the cliff in the valley floor of Santa Fe Canyon.

Figure 57. Ink drawing of Uretsete and Naotsete wrestling.

The panel describes the relationship of this animal as a metaphor for Naotsete, mother of the Navajo. It is the symbol belonging to the "outside" realm of Keresan society, the domain of the hunting and war societies.

Farther down Santa Fe Canyon a few yards is another panel depicting Uretsete and Naotsete. They are identified by their hair whorls and body shapes. Their hands are poised again in wrestling postures. This panel simply reiterates the conflict that is the central theme within the myth, i.e., who has the right to populate the land to the south. Both figures have open spread legs so as not to be mistaken as anything other than two females. Naotsete is identified by the labia of her genitals that appear in previous renditions of her. Uretsete is below her but the symbol of procreation (a penis) has been added. Together, these symbols depict a struggle (wrestling) over the right to procreate (penis) between the two sisters. Figure 56 is a photograph of this panel. Figure 57 is an ink rendering of this panel.

This panel could convey another level of information that pertains to the cosmological relationship that Uretsete and Naotsete bring into being. In Keresan oral traditions, Uretsete is at times portrayed as a male deity. Anthony Purley, like Boas, believed that "the trend to refer to Uretsete as male is a late development and may reflect a Keres gesture to white tastes in deities. Uretsete is not always male, even in present-day narratives or sacred myths, but changes gender midstream, as it were" (Allen 1987:271).

Uretsete as a deity and a metaphor may represent the spiritual realities that penetrate the material realities. Naotsete, on some level, may represent the outside forces that include materialism, politics, and warfare. Together, the two deities create a balance with a dynamic interaction. Uretsete is the inner force representing the internal structure of Keresan world views, which in turn, is masked by Naotsete on the outside representing the outer form as presented to the outside world.

In this panel Uretsete lies horizontal, in line with the Earth, the mother of all people, the place of emergence and life substance, of dreams, visions and the unconscious mind. Naotsete stands upright, aligned with the material realms, the physical, the conscious mind, the outer image put forth for the public eye, and alien encounters. Uretsete below, is penetrating Naotsete above, as a metaphor for the spirituality that penetrates all aspects of pueblo society. Together, Uretsete and Naotsete are the essence of the dualities that make up the rhythms of the cosmos.

END NOTES

1. Leslie White (1932b:56 n,68) notes: "There is an animal called Ck'a'wac which looks `like a big rat' (I could not identify it), which is sometimes caught by the boys when rabbit hunting. They bring them home, but the G'o'watca'nyi do not gather them along with the rabbits because, it is said, the Ck'a'wac is the mother of their old time enemy, the Navajo. It is said to be the mother of the Navajo because it makes a nest of shredded cedar bark for its young, just as a Navajo woman makes a nest for her baby."

6
THE IARIKO PANEL

Ts'its'tsi'nako, Thought-Woman,
is sitting in her room
and whatever she thinks about
appears.
She thought of her sisters,
Nau'ts'ity'i and I'tcts'ity'i,
and together they created the Universe
this world
and the four worlds below.
Thought-Woman, the spider,
named things and
as she named them
they appeared.
She is sitting in her room
thinking of a story now.
I am telling you the story
she is thinking.

_____Keresan Poem (Silko 1977:1)

Continuing along the cliff, to the right of the Uretsete and Naotsete panel, is the final panel depicting Spider, Uretsete and the corn fetish, the *Iariko*. This panel elaborates on the creation of the Iariko and Uretsete's relationship to the Sipapu, Spider, and the Iariko. The Iariko panel is shown in Plate 8.

Dumarest (1919:216) describes some of this relationship:

Uretsete had planned an Iariko. She wound thongs of deer hide about an ear of corn and placed at its top feathers of a turkey which at her order had shaken out its feathers for her. But finding that her work was not perfect, she had called to Spider, saying to him [her], "I have wished to make for my people something endowed with the same power as myself, and to give it to them. I know that you are thoughtful. How does my work seem to you?" Spider said, "It is good, but put at the top some parrot feathers and at the neck some eagle-down, and all will be well." Uretsete did this, and thus was created the Iariko, which she gave to the two men sent by the emigrants. She said to the two, after having initiated them into the mysteries of the `Chaiani'. "This has the same power as I. Take it to my people, that the sick may recover health".

An Iariko is made from a perfect ear of corn. Eagle feathers and down are placed around the corn. Parrot feathers are placed at the top. Wooden splints, used to keep the feathers positioned, are woven in place with cotton cord. The inside of the corn ear is carved out and an obsidian "heart" is placed within it. The Iariko has a "face" painted on the tip end. Parrot feathers are placed in the back of the "head." A turquoise and obsidian-beaded necklace is put around the Iariko's "neck." Iarikos are the most sacred of Keres idols.[1] Plate 9 is a photograph of an Iariko from Matilda Cox Stevenson's illustration of a Sia (now referred to as Zia Pueblo) Corn Mother fetish in her article "The Sia" in *Eleventh Annual Report of the Bureau of American Ethnology 1889-90* of the Smithsonian Institution.

SYMBOL IDENTIFICATION

In the petroglyph panel there is a large drawing of the corn fetish with feathers attached all around it that represent the Iariko. It also has a small round "head" that personifies this fetish, which the Pueblo call the "Corn Mother." It is positioned next to a corn plant, identified by the bend and droop of the long leaves. The proximity to each other demonstrates the relationship between corn fetish and corn plant. The Eastern and Western Pueblos say the Corn Mother fetish is "made from a perfect ear of corn."

Uretsete is identified in this panel by her hair whorls. She is positioned below and to the side of the corn fetish, touching it with her hand to denote her association with it. Uretsete is positioned near her "abode below" as symbolized by the terraced image that represents the Sipapu below her.

Figure 58.   Ink drawing of the Iariko panel.

Figure 58 is a graphic illustration of the Iariko panel. Notice that the panel is bisected by a distinct crack. Part of the Corn Mother fetish projects above the horizontal crack. Uretsete, the bird with the one cross-foot, Spider and the Sipapu are positioned below the horizontal crack. The positioning of these images, both below and protruding above the crack, defines the realms to which each character now belongs, that of the underworld and the above world. Uretsete has returned to her abode below and has given her people the Iariko to communicate with her. Through the Iariko, or Corn Mother, Uretsete will know all of her people's thoughts and prayers. Stevenson (1894:40) relates more of the story:

> I, Uretsete, will soon leave you. I will return to the home whence I came. You will be to my people as myself; you will pass with them over the straight road, I will remain in my house below and will hear all that you say to me. I give to you all my wisdom, my thoughts, my heart, and all. I fill your head with my mind.

In the petroglyph panel, the line leading out the top of the Iariko and leading down from the bottom to the Sipapu may indicate the "pathway" of communication from Uretsete, through the Iariko to the people. Uretsete has turkey-track hands that indicate the direction of travel, in reference to her wisdom, her thoughts, her heart, and all, from herself through the corn fetish to her people.

Uretsete's other symbol, the bird with one cross-foot, is also present. As previously explained, Uretsete and the bird occur together in every panel throughout the entire sequence. This consistency supports the conviction that Uretsete in her human form and the bird form are one in the same entity.

Below this panel is a flat ledge that still has traces of cornmeal left as offerings to Spider (Thought Woman), Uretsete (Earth Mother) and the Iariko (Corn Mother). Joe Herrera from Cochiti Pueblo pointed out that the physical context of the ledge below this panel creates a natural altar for Uretsete. It is here, he gestured, that the offerings are made to "Our Mother" and this is her shrine.

Chart 6 is the etic and emic analysis of this panel, integrating the two perspectives for the final interpretation.

CONCLUSIONS

It is told in the myth that Uretsete creates the corn fetish to represent her in a physical form. The corn fetish is made with a head, a heart, a body, feathers, and a perfect ear of corn as described by White and Stevenson.[1] The petroglyph emphasizes the fetish's head, neck, body, and appendages as a partly human, partly corn-and-feather object.

The three entities, Uretsete, Spider, and the Iariko, become the essential participants within Keresan cosmology. Uretsete remains below in the Sipapu. She becomes known as Earth Woman (Iyatikyu). Spider becomes known as Thought Woman, (Tse che nako) and continues to assist Uretsete with inspiration. The Iariko becomes Corn Mother, (Irriaku) the physical manifestation of Uretsete. Paula Allen (1986:22) writes:

> As the power of woman is the center of the universe and is both heart (womb) and thought (creativity), the power of the Keres people is the corn that holds the thought of the ALL power (deity) and connects the people to that power through the heart of Earth Woman, Iyatikyu. She is the breath of life to the Keres because for them corn holds the essence of earth and conveys the power of earth to the people.

Spider is called by various names; Tse che nako, Tsityostinako, Tsichtinako, Sussistinnako, and Ts'its'ts'ciinaak'o. These names have been translated as Spider Man (Dumarest); Spider Woman by several others; Creator, Prophesying Woman (White); and Thought Woman and Creating-Through-Thinking Woman (Allen). This deity sang the two sisters into being, and then taught them the rituals to use to sing everything else into being.

Uretsete eventually leaves the people and goes to the Sipapu. Allen (1986) believes this is the dream/vision center of the tribe's ritual life, from whence Uretsete guides the people. She is aided by the *cacique* and counseled by the Spirit of Thought, Spider Woman, who sits near her or on her shoulder and whispers in her ear.

The panel confirms the verbal description of this relationship between Spider and Uretsete with the spatial arrangement in the panel of Spider, low and to the side of Uretsete with one arm touching her. Uretsete is drawn in the center to "receive knowledge and advice" from Spider. Uretsete is touching the corn fetish to her other side, representing the connecting element between these deities and the human world.

Uretsete represents the "heart of the people." The present-day caciques continue to act as her representative and gain their power directly from her. Corn connects to the heart of power, Uretsete, who is under the guidance of Spider (Thought Woman) and directs the people in their affairs. Corn, like many of its power counterparts in other Indian cultures, is responsible for maintaining a linkage between the worlds; and the Corn Mother, the Iariko, is the most powerful element in that link. The Corn Mother fetish plays an important part in the ritual life of the pueblo. It is the embodiment of power that moves between the material and spiritual worlds.[2]

It is important to remember that myths and metaphors are not literal events and images. Metaphor has a unique language of its own. Levi-Strauss (1988:186-187) states:

> A metaphor always works both ways....it is like a two-way street. In switching terms that belong to different codes, the metaphor rests on an intuition that these terms connote the same semantic field when seen from a more global perspective. The metaphor restores this semantic field.

Myth has the ability of being mutually convertible.[3] The meaning of the metaphors found in this myth are in a code that cannot be translated literally, but can be converted instead to another code. This allows us to understand an unfamiliar code in terms of a more familiar code.

An example of what happens when a metaphor is reduced to a literal translation is demonstrated with a comparison of interpretations of Tse che nako or Spider Woman, Thought Woman or Creating-through-Thinking Woman (Allen (1986). Tse che nako has been called "Prophesying Woman" (White 1962:113) because "she knows, rather than deciding or determining what will happen." Most of the literature suggests that this deity represents the origin of thought and intuitive thinking. In Pueblo Indian societies the *source* of thought is believed to be from the "heart," metaphorically speaking, which also represents the source of truth, knowledge and creativity. To most Indian cultures, the metaphor for expressing truth is stated as something "coming from the heart," and a truthful and knowledgeable person is one who "speaks from the heart." This metaphor is important because it distinguishes between thoughts that are consciously derived, and perhaps egotistical, and those that are intuitively derived and more spiritually aligned.

Miller (1989), in contrast, has translated Tse che nako to mean "Consciousness Deity"[4] creating a semantic conflict. The term "consciousness" refers to the brain as a metaphor in Western cultures. The metaphors of brain and heart are not interchangeable and the Western European metaphor of the "mind" as "consciousness" has been imposed on the Keresan concept of intuitive thinking, and "knowing" associated with the heart metaphor.

Miller uses "Deity," rather than "woman" to further deny gender and the metaphoric attributes associated to women. The ending "-nako" in Keresan means woman and as a metaphor, is necessary to fulfill the role of a creator, who like a woman can bring new life into the world. The contrast of interpretations is important because it points up the difficulties which are recurrent in any analysis or discussion of symbolism associated with a high context culture.

ENDNOTES

1. Stevenson (1894: 40) describes the corn fetish: " The Iariko or ya'ya (mother) is an ear of corn which may be any color but must be symmetrically perfect, and not a grain must be missing. Eagle and parrot plumes are placed in pyramidal form around the corn. In order that the center feathers may be sufficiently long they are each attached to a very delicate splint. The base of this pyramid is formed of splints woven together with native cotton cord and ornamented at the top with shells and precious beads. A pad of native cotton is attached to the lower end of the corn. When the Iariko is complete there is no evidence of the corn... The Iariko is Sia's supreme idol."

Leslie White (1962:307-309), in a later documentation of Sia Pueblo, writes, "Iariko (or Iatiku) is `the Mother of all the Indians' in Keresan mythology (Utstsiti, in our Sia myth is equated with Iariko). This fetish consists of a decorated ear of corn... The ear of corn used must be perfect, with straight rows and fully kerneled to the tip. Feathers of the wren, especially, but also magpie, roadrunner, turkey, duck or mocking bird are glued to the ear with honey of the bumblebee. The pith of the cob is removed from the butt end about half way to the tip. Into this cavity the `heart' is inserted. This may be either a small round black stone called Dyatca'aicti or a bit of quartz crystal (witcatsi)... Then a number of narrow strips of bamboo are cut in lengths of the corn ear. Each is wrapped with cotton string, and at the top end a fluffy eagle feather, taken from beneath the tail, is tied. These slats are then placed longitudinally alongside the ear of corn. They are securely held with a wooden hoop at the top and bottom of the ear. Then parrot tail feathers are inserted in the top of the fetish, inside the circle of eagle feathers. The fetish has a `face' on one side of the tip end. At the back of the 'head' two long parrot feathers are inserted. A necklace of turquoise, obsidian, and beads is placed around Iariko's 'neck'. Iarikos are placed upright upon the altars during ceremonies, always facing the door."

2. Allen (1986:19) writes," It is through the agency of the Iariko that the religious leaders of the tribe, called Yaya and Hotchin, or Hochin (mother and leader of chief) are empowered to govern. The Irriaku (Iariko), like the Sacred Pipe of the Lakota, is the heart of the people as it is the heart of Iyatiku, (Uretsete). In the form of the perfect ear of corn, Naiya Iyatikuy (Mother, Chief) is present at every ceremony. Without the presence of her power, no ceremony can produce the power it is designated to create or release."

3. "The signification of a myth is always global; it cannot be reduced to the interpretation provided by one particular code. No language - astronomical, sexual, or other conveys the `better' meaning...There is no more truth in one code than in any other. The essence of the myth is founded on the property inherent in all codes: that of being mutually convertible." (Levi-Strauss 1988:186-187)

Mando Sevillano (1986) comments on the Hopi version of Spider Woman: " According to the narrator, the mere mention of Spider Woman, to a Hopi, means that you can breathe easily. There is help. Everything is okay. Probably a wise old person popping up in a tense circumstance is a comfort to anyone anywhere, for this person offers something definite in an indefinite situation. The appearance of Navajo Kachina Uncle is comforting, says the narrator, but the appearance of Spider Woman, in the Hopi way, is an analog to the appearance of Christ, the Holy Spirit, or an angel in the Christian way."

4. Jay Miller (1990) makes a case for the identification of Spider Woman in what he terms "Consciousness Deity." Miller states: "The first part of the name refers to conscious mental activity or awareness, so I will refer to T (Tse che nako) as Consciousness Deity....Manly is regarded as marked and exclusive, while Womanly is unmarked and inclusive. They are bound together by a shared property of Mind, as thought, consciousness, or intelligence. So pervasive are these categories that animals are described in myth and ritual as humanoids wearing skin cloaks. The mediation of Mind as the inclusive category is deified as Consciousness Deity, the head of the Keres pantheon...."

7
PETROGLYPH INTERPRETATION
Yesterday, Today, and Tomorrow

A great number of prehistoric panels reveal a high percentage of battle accounts, disputes, and migrations. Their full value, however, cannot be realized until tribal identities are established and until the ancient idioms [metaphors] of these panels can be thoroughly understood in the light of the cultural backgrounds in which they were used.

———La Van Martineau.

YESTERDAY

In the last century, several scholars investigating Indian petroglyphs concluded that the petroglyphs contained symbols that comprised a type of communication system based in some way on the Indian sign language as it was used in a relatively universal fashion by most tribes in this country. Mallery published a lengthy volume on the Picture Writing of the American Indians as did Schoolcraft on the elements of the pictorial system of the American Indians in volume 1 of his work. Publication of the scrolls of the Midewiwin Medicine society, and the Walum Olum are also classified as "picture writing" that entailed a code system. Fewkes describes the Hopi "picture writing" as pictography in his article, "A Few Tusayan Pictographs." He defines pictographs as a picture writing system utilizing symbols. This definition has changed in time to mean only images painted on rocks, as opposed to pecked images on rocks (petroglyphs).

Historically, the Europeans gave up picture writing, or the picturing of ideas, as a communication system for another system that is abstracted one step further. Alphabetic symbol systems represent sounds that, when put together as words, represent ideas. These words are generally specific to a single language, hence the meaning of each word is common knowledge only to the speakers of that particular language.

The Indian picture writing system, on the other hand, has never presented symbols for sounds in association with any one language. It has retained an interpretability that is relatively cross-lingual. It transmits ideas through a symbolic language that bypasses the verbal language specific to one culture or tribe. Thus, Indian groups of various languages could interpret, to some degree, a general message portrayed on the rocks. Scholars and cavalry officers of the last century realized that it was possible to cross more widely separated cultural lines, as between Indian and European cultures, if an effort was made to view the writing emically from a Indian perspective. Attempting an interpretation of Indian petroglyphs requires a major effort to understand the highly contextual information by means of ethnography and metaphorical information.

TODAY

Scholars of a European mind-set will always have difficulty interpreting petroglyph symbols using their linear thinking system that is associated with alphabetic writing. Historically, the mechanistic theory of the universe, formulated in the Newtonian physics age, has provided the Western European with a mythic mind set proposing that the universe is composed of small, solid objects called atoms, floating and interacting in an absolute void.

> Mechanistic science is an example of the success of a particular mythic mode of consciousness that has been carried forward with great energy, dedication, and commitment by many people (Europeans)....Examples of radically different modes that have achieved success in their own spheres of endeavor are shamanism and yoga. Shamans, operating within a frame of their own mythic consciousness, travel to other worlds, act as guides to departing souls at death and heal the sick with methods that make no sense to physicians trained in the American Medical Association- approved medical schools. The yogi, developing a mastery over the inner world comparable to the mastery of modern science over the outer, objective world, may be visited by siddhis, or powers, which appear to be miraculous. Neither shaman nor yogi finds reality limited by scientific theories, no matter how those theories might deny their experiences.
>
> Combs and Holland 1990:XX

The 20th century has seen the development of new scientific world views with the general theories of relativity and quantum physics. Both are congenial to a philosophy of wholeness and interrelatedness that is similar to and less in contrast with the Indian world view. Yet it takes time for these new world views to take hold in academic circles and within the general populace. By understanding of the European linear mind set, one can perhaps understand the difficulty most readers have with interpreting Indian petroglyphs that represent a different world view.

> Rock art and traditional art are interested in presenting the world as it is. That view is not always linear, in concept, and in many cases will appear to be more subjective than objective... Their psychic frame of reference was founded on an understanding of the principles of natural law, which include a holistic division of earth and life.
>
> Frank La Pena in Tilberg 1983:25

94

The dominant culture, in this country, gives high priority to low-context information-gathering systems. In order to better understand indigenous cultures, there must instead be a serious inquiry made into the emic world view and high cultural context. An attitude of "get what information seems important fast and efficiently" lacks the total involvement and time-consuming contexting, which are both necessary requirements for the study of petroglyph symbols.

A truly successful key to petroglyph interpretation has eluded researchers of the present century, and their theories have since drifted from a concept of symbolic communication to one of primarily artistic or pictorial representation. Most scholars today believe there is not enough evidence to support the theory of a pictographic writing system. Perhaps it is more a problem of understanding the evidence rather than the lack of it. One could compare a natural symbol system, such as dress code, between Europeans and Indians (Douglas 1982). Indian ceremonial attire contains highly contextual symbolism, that denotes an individual's social position, lineage, philosophy, etc., whereas European formal attire contains few if any symbols with the exception of military status. The traditional black tie affair is typical of a "non-associative" culture, whereas a pow wow with traditional dress codes is an expression of a very "associative" culture (Edward T. Hall; May 15, 1989 personal conversation). Jane Young noted this aspect also with her experience with Zuni Trade Fairs, where the colors, symbols, rituals, and pageantry are rich in cultural context and uniquely different from mainstream culture.[1] How does a person of a low context culture ever fully understand the meaning of the symbols from a highly contexted culture? Perhaps one's understanding can only be limited and one must be content with that, considering the study itself is an on-going process that never achieves completion, only enrichment as it evolves.

The work of La Van Martineau is founded upon the theories of the earlier scholars regarding the visual and conceptual relationship between petroglyphs and Indian Sign Language. The fundamental differences between European world views and those of the Rio Grande Pueblo Indian further become apparent when culturally specific metaphors are examined more closely. The potential of the study of Indian sign language to aid petroglyph interpretation is outlined in the charts that follow each chapter.

The correspondence between Keresan and Tewa (or Rio Grande Pueblo) myths and the petroglyph panels located within the study area of the La Cienega Pueblo site illustrate how Martineau's methods help to elucidate the subject and purpose of the panels. The examples given of petroglyphs from other culture areas illustrate the principles of spatial syntax, symbol combination and so on, but are not presented to suggest a pan-cultural or cross-cultural symbol identification. Some symbol meanings may change from tribe to tribe within a culture area, i.e., Pueblos are found in both Eastern and Western areas. Within the Eastern Pueblos, the Keres and Tewa have differences in some symbol identifications. Within the Keresan culture, certain villages may discriminate between each other. And so on to the individual informant who may contradict other individual informants depending upon their social status and occupation. What is pan-cultural and cross-cultural is the structure of the symbol system. Using that as a guide, a close association between the myths and the symbols can be postulated.

One purpose of this book is to show the results of employing Martineau's methods on a group of pueblo petroglyphs to demonstrate how it has helped to substantiate the remarkable correspondence between these interpretations and the myths of the pueblo people. As a result, one can safely say the myths are written on the rocks and one can interpret much of what is there.

For many years the enigmatic nature of American Indian petroglyphs has intrigued and puzzled European observers. Interpretation is difficult. Even with Martineau's methods, the interpretation process will vary from one researcher to another, as each formulates a slightly different approach and defines the symbol meanings according to the information one has personally gathered. One must be prepared to accept the nature of high context cultures, in which there are multiple meanings, multiple variations of oral traditions and multiple levels of interpretation. No one interpretation is the only right one. Many variations occur, yet together they may convey, "all the same thing."

This book is written in a progressive, linear format to present information within a structure more familiar to most readers. It is hoped that they will realize that when reading a petroglyph panel, the interpretation progression often follows a flow pattern that appears to meander about the panel. Its progression is often influenced by the physical nature of the rock surface and availability of surface areas. The flow patterns for some of the panels discussed in this book are shown in Figures 59, 60, 61.

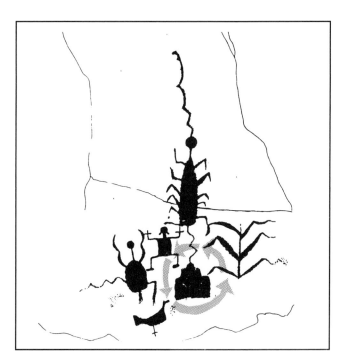

Figure 59.   Flow pattern of the Iariko panel

Figure 60.   Flow pattern of Uretsete and Naotsete panels.

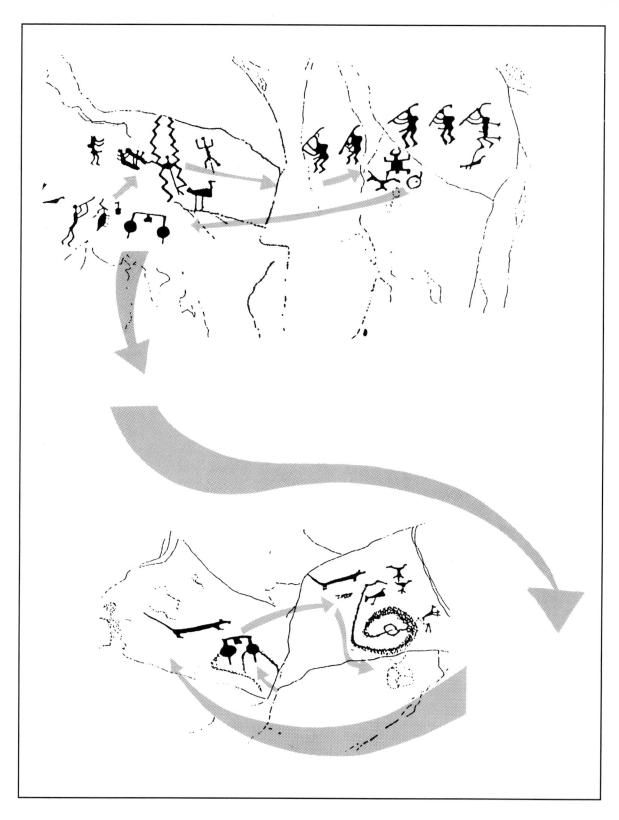

Figure 61. Flow pattern of Water Jar Boy panels.

FUTURE OF PETROGLYPH INTERPRETATION

Classification of petroglyph symbols as style or artistic categories is of limited value. These kinds of surveys tend to take the symbols out of context and classify them in terms of an ethnocentric observation. The quadrupeds, for example, become identified as "species" or species-like, rather than considered a symbol or sign vehicle interrelated with other symbols in context with each other. Future studies should be conducted in a more holistic manner, in which the petroglyph panel and site are recorded inclusive of rock formations; cracks; patination; overhangs; directional orientation; proximity to trails, streams or bodies of water; food sources; plants and animal habitat; and, human settlement remains. All these are especially important for the purposes of symbol interpretation by future investigators.

The consideration of metaphorical meanings for specific petroglyph symbols as metaphors, metonymies, and sign vehicles demonstrated throughout this book and can open the way for a deeper understanding of other Indian petroglyphs of a similar nature. Identifying symbols in a petroglyph panel as metaphors is possible with the careful study of indigenous cultural metaphors.

It has been shown how metaphors clearly distinguish some of the subtle differences between Pueblo Indian culture and European culture which at times has resulted in gross misunderstandings. The concepts that people communicate to each other are structured individually, from the metaphors they use. A concept can fall short or be extended by the imagery contained in the metaphor chosen in conversation. Lakoff and Johnson (1986:136) say that:

> Metaphors in the conceptual system indicate coherent and systematic relationships between concepts. The use of the same words and grammatical devices for concepts with systematic metaphorical correspondences (like time and space) is one way in which the correspondence between form and meaning in a language are 'logical' rather than arbitrary."

The metaphors of the mountain lion, the double-lobed jar, the spring, and the water serpent logically explain the boy's "hero journey." Uretsete is represented by a bird as a metaphor to convey the spiritual aspects of her being. Spider Woman as a metaphor can convey creative, intuitive, and knowledgeable aspects of a Creator Deity. In metaphors, then, the conceptualization of the non-physical is grounded in the physical, a natural world that is familar to the pueblo.

Metonymies are synechodoches that serve the same purpose as metaphors, but focus more specifically on certain aspects of what is being represented. The part for the whole, a track for an animal, or an animal for a person, his nature or role, are examples as explored in this book.

Sign Vehicles are composed of a basic symbol, such as a man, a bird, or an animal, with additional symbols added on. The add-on symbols may modify the head, or body or appendages on the body as shown in Chart 2 with the quadruped, and in Chapter 4 with the human figure with turkey-track hands. These add-ons are derived from basic sign language gestures, that convey various physical ideas such as directional movement, action, evasion, aggression, and geographical location. Emotional expressions, that are displayed on the human face with position of eyebrows, up (happy), down (mad), and outward (sad), are displayed by "extensions" using ears or antenna on a petroglyph figure. These extensions of human ears, are found drawn straight up, to express "awareness" or "looking for." They are found drawn in a relaxed position, the meaning implied is "unaware." Together these facial extensions, such as antenna, clarify the intent of the figure.

The symbol combinations and their syntactic arrangements, which are made up of the basic symbols found in Chart 7, can be disassembled and discussed on several levels that depend upon cultural context information. The spring, for example, in Chapter 3 is a symbol combination that involves cultural concepts, such as *the Center Place,* a *serpent* in the spring, and the *spiritual realm.* The Iariko contains basic symbols that represent the head, the body, and the appendages. But the cultural context of *Corn Mother* is necessary to understand the full meaning of this image.

The importance of viewing petroglyph symbols metaphorically cannot be over-stated. Without a metaphorical interpretation, the presence of the Indian myths in the La Cienega petroglyphs could not have been reasonably demonstrated.

The overall significance of the interpretations put forth in this book provides a better understanding of cultural, visual, and communicative elements in petroglyphs. Potentially this will tell more about social and demographic change in prehistory and strongly augments contemporary oral traditions. Archaeological interest should be stimulated as well if corroborating evidence of different material cultures can be found to correspond with the pictographic record of migrational movements or direct accounts of religious or cosmological beliefs. The multivalence of symbols in these panels in conjunction with the metaphors of the myths represent a dynamic, living tradition of great value, yet many secrets as to the full meaning of the panels are still undiscovered.

ENDNOTES

1. Young 1988:107): "Zuni costumes, altars, religious paraphernalia, ceremonial rooms, pottery, wall murals and the ritual activity itself are all replete with sensory images — objects, sounds, colors, and so on — repeated over and over again, all resonating, all dense with meaning, frequently referring to "the same thing." Although I have listed examples that relate to religious life, my observations of "secular" activities such as the Zuni Tribal Fair lead to the same conclusions. Secular costumes, exhibit rooms for the fair, the fairground itself, floats in the parade, social dances and music, all are characterized by layers and layers of symbols, colors, and sounds, all bound together metaphorically.".

2. Martineau (1984) comments: "There are probably some similar minor differences in the rock writings of different Indian tribes, but they cannot be fully discerned or evaluated until the system can be read in its entirety. The apparent noticeable differences in style are really a difference in topic as already explained and really does not reflect upon the structure of the writing system itself."

CHART 1   QUADRUPED BREAKDOWNS

Sign Language Metaphor:	Movement	Covered	Open	Blocked
Heads and Horns:	Heading Movement	Emerging Coming out	Returning	Rough Difficult
Body:	Place Here Land	Valley Bowl Below	Hill Mountain Above	Around Side	Canyon Eye
Body Posture:	Going	Going up	Going down	Dead
Legs:	Standing Staying	Going Walking	Veering Avoiding Giving up Turned aside	Not turned aside Resisting

CHART 2   FLUTE PLAYERS

Locust Kokopelli

Bandelier   SW Pueblo   Zuni   Cienegilla   Cienegilla   Cienegilla

Human Flute Players

Flute Players
wife hunting
Cienegilla

Flute Players

Same Panel
La Cienegilla

3 different postures of flute players
1. Wife hunter's backpack, ceremonial belt, antenna, and feather
2. Fertility figure, phallus, backpack, arms gesturing, no head, no flute
3. flute player, no backpack, no phallus, no antenna

Burden basket, backpack
side by side in the same Panel
Cienegilla

Cloud Blower
La Cienega

Flute Player - a cloud blower
Pointed back - burden basket
Cienegilla

104

		"Mixing water": water+person+splash up inside
		"Wet person rising up": particles + person + rising up of something from knees (moisture) kneeling
		"Spring": particles + descend, of something or snake (moisture) or spring Spring + center place
		"Growing up": moisture + dry + horn + quadruped moving upward
		"Descend to place": turkey tracks down + place or land or person
		"Iariko, Corn Mother": head and body + ear of corn + feathers + pathway

CHART 4   WATER JAR BOY

Panel

Symbol Description	Flute players, ceremonial belts, phalluses	Horned figure in birthing position
	Thing with two appendages	Round thing
Symbol Combinations	None	
Sign Language Body Posture	Traveling Playing flutes	Strong horns Birthing
Spatial Syntax Spatial Positioning	Movement in one direction No connection with female	Object under legs of female
Myth Constituent Units	A fine girl did not want to marry any of the boys. Boys from other villages heard about her. She would not marry any boy.	After some days she felt something in her belly. She had a baby. It was a round thing with two things sticking out, a little jar.
Interpretation in Mythic Context	Suitors traveling in search for wife, carrying bridal goods. None are stopping or interacting with maiden.	Maiden gives birth to abnormal object that is round with appendages.

WATER JAR BOY

Panel

Symbol Identification	Phallic figure Seed pack on back	Arms and legs of figure are in water, mixing mud Water symbol Splashing water into figure	Leaving Turned away
Symbol Combinations		 Water + Man + Pathway + Foot kicking Pathway leading into body	
Sign Language Body Posture	Beckoning Arm gesture	Copulating couple	Bird turned away
Spatial Syntax Spatial Positioning	Facing couple	Connected to water symbol	Facing away from other symbols but close proximity
Myth Constituent Units	Mother asked daughter to mix clay, using one foot to stamp it.	Girl felt mud splash up her leg.	Mother left to go for water.
Interpretation in Mythic Context	Fertility	Conception by water	Bird (mother) leaving daughter

107

WATER JAR BOY

Panel

Symbol Description	Flute player sign vehicle	Double-lobed jar

Symbol Combinations		Dry horn Wet horn Quadruped moving upwards

Sign Language Body Posture	Flute player gesturing upward	Vertical position of quadruped

Spatial Syntax Spatial Positioning	flute player gesturing up towards copulating couple	Proximity to double lobed jar

Myth Constituent Units

Mother and her father are surprised. Father is glad to have a grandson.

Water jar is growing and can talk. It is fed through the mouth.

It tells them it is a boy.
The boy grows up inside the jar.

Interpretation in Mythic Context	Singing to life with flute player	Moving up (growing) from watery to dry place	World of duality Darkness Unconscious mind

WATER JAR BOY

Panel		
Symbol Identification	Mountain lion/boy	Double-lobed jar/water jar Water leaking out.
Symbol Combinations	wet	boy
Sign Language Body Posture	Boy raising up on knees.	Mountain lion facing double-lobed jar.	Jar depicted with dotted particles coming from sides.
Spatial Syntax Spatial Positioning	Boy positioned near mountain lion and jar.		Moisture coming out of sides of jar instead of the top.
Myth Constituent Units	Boy asks to go hunting. Grandfather takes him. Mother cries because he has no arms or legs. Boy goes hunting	He rolls after a rabbit. He hits a rock and breaks Boy emerges from broken jar.
Interpretation in Mythic Context	Boy goes hunting, like "a mountain lion." Boy breaks out of his world.	He defies what others say can not be done.

WATER JAR BOY

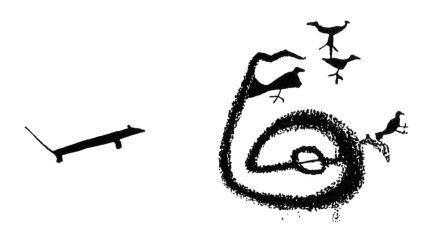

Symbol Description	Mountain lion	Coil	Birds
Symbol Combination	⟨descend⟩	⟨wet⟩	⟨snake⟩
Sign Language Body Posture	Mountain lion heading towards coil.		Bird with large breast.
Spatial Syntax Spatial Positioning	Mountain lion near coil. Open center at end of coil.		Birds at top of coil.
Myth Constituent Units	Boy goes in search of his (supernatural) father. Boy goes to a spring. They both descend into the spring.	He meets a man there. After several trials, the man admits he is the boy's father. The boy meets his relatives.	
Interpretation in Mythic Context	Boy goes in search, (like a mountain lion) for his spiritual father. The water serpent is his father.	He arrives at the Spring. He descends to the "Center Place" and meets all his relatives. His mother dies and rejoins him in the Spring.	

CHART 5

URETSETE AND NAOTSETE

Panel		
Symbol Description	Sign vehicle depicting movement downward.	Two female figures with maiden hair whorls and arms in active gestures.
Symbol Combinations	Turkey tracks + Human body	
Sign Language Body Posture	Motion downward Gesture for struggle	Gesture for help
Spatial Syntax Spatial Positioning	Sign vehicle positioned above two female figures.	Two females positioned at very bottom of Panel.
Myth Constituent Units	Uretsete, smaller, mother of all Indians.	Naotsete, larger, Mother of all Aliens.
	Challenge each other to a contest of powers for the privilege to people the land to the south.	Descend to the park to fight, not with weapons but wrestled.
Interpretation in Mythic Context	Uretsete and Naotsete challenge each other to a contest of powers.	They descend to the park below to fight.

URETSETE AND NAOTSETE

Panel

Symbol Description	Snake	Bird with one cross-foot.	Arrow heads
	Corn meal trail	Birds with feet touching a crack.	

Symbol Combinations

Snake   +   dotted particles.

Spatial Syntax Spatial Positioning	Snake in proximity with birds. Arrow touching first and second bird's head.	Arrow touching third bird's foot. Bird's feet touching crack. No arrow touching fourth bird.

Myth Constituent Units	Contest naming bird tracks, of Crow, Roadrunner, Turkey, and Snake, in a road of corn meal.	Confusion over the Roadrunner track.
		No mistake over "name" or "track" of last bird.
	Uretsete puts line of corn meal across snake's forehead.	

Interpretation in Mythic Context	Uretsete is challenged to name the different bird tracks. She is represented by the bird with one cross-foot.	Conflict is represented by arrow heads.
		Snake is making a track through the corn meal, represented by dots.
	Conflict over the bird tracks is represented by the arrow touching the bird's foot.	Snake is blessed by Uretsete with a line of cornmeal across its head.

112

URETSETE AND NAOTSETE

Panel			
Symbol Description	Bird with one cross-foot.	two triangles bare foot print	striated half circle dotted line
Sign Language Body Posture	Bare foot print	Tracks going up.	
Spatial Syntax Spatial Positioning	Bird with one cross-foot near arrow points and track.	Bare foot print touching arrow.	Dotted line leading from one symbol, to another symbol.
Myth Constituent Units	People divide into two sides and make arrows in preparation for a fight.	Two women go to the top of a hill at dawn. Both wear an eagle feather.	
	Magpie spreads his wing over the sun shading the taller feather and illuminating the lower feather.		
Interpretation in Mythic Context	Bird with one cross-foot represents Uretsete. Bare foot print represents people preparing for battle. Dotted line is pathway of sunlight going to lower feather tip.	Triangles represent feathers. Tracks of Uretsete and Naotsete going to top of hill. Magpie wing is striated symbol.	

URETSETE AND NAOTSETE

Panel

| **Symbol Description** | Small feet | Bird wing | Pack rat |
| | Large feet | Penis | Human legs and arm |

| **Symbol Combinations** | Wing | Pack rat | Penis | Human feet |

| **Sign Language Body Posture** | feet separated
feet connected | Wing touching
heart position. | Legs in "separation"
gesture. |

Arm gesture for "distant."
Hand touching penis indicates "procreation."

| **Spatial Syntax Spatial Positioning** | Smaller feet above.
Larger feet below,
indicated domination. | Bird wing touching
"heart" position of
other figure. |

| **Myth Constituent Units** | Uretsete calls for help
to save herself. Naotsete
is tied up. | Uretsete cuts out Naotsete's
heart, splits it in half
into a squirrel and a dove. |

Naotsete predicts all future sons
and daughters "will be just like ourselves."

| **Interpretation in Mythic Context** | Uretsete over came Naotsete. | Heart is split in two. |

Heart turns into a dove and a pack rat.

Naotsete predicts future (distant), generations (procreation),
to be the same as both of themselves.

URETSETE AND NAOTSETE

Panel

| **Symbol Description** | Bird with one cross-foot.

The crack is a symbol. | Dog or Coyote touching a crack. |

Symbol Combination

wet + bird
"spirit"

Sign Language Body Posture

Repetition of the Bird with one cross-foot.
Change of appearance or transformation of some kind.

Spatial Syntax Spatial Positioning

Movement in lateral direction.
Movement in downward direction.

| **Myth Constituent Units** | Uretsete goes to Sipapu underground.

People fall into ill ways and send Coyote to ask Uretsete for help. | Coyote talks to Uretsete in underworld. |

| **Interpretation in Mythic Context** | Bird with one cross-foot represents Uretsete descending down the crack, or pathway that goes to the Sipapu. | Coyote talks to her through the crack that leads to the underworld. |

URETSETE AND NAOTSETE

Panel

Symbol Identification	Ear of corn with a feather. Bird with beak touching feather.	Bird with foot touching feather.
Symbol Combination	Birds and a feather Ear of corn and a feather	
Sign Language Body Posture	Bird "head" = talking, asking, eating. Bird "foot" = walking, getting, giving.	
Spatial Syntax Spatial Positioning	One bird "head" touching and the other bird "foot" touching the same object.	
Mythic Constituent Units	Uretsete plans an Iariko using an ear of corn, and feathers of Turkey, who gave them at her request.	Other birds give her feathers at her command.
Interpretation in Mythic Context	Uretsete makes the Iariko from a perfect ear of corn. She asks other birds for feathers.	She asks for feathers from Turkey, the first bird, who gives them willingly.

CHART 7
BASIC SYMBOLS

Iconic symbols

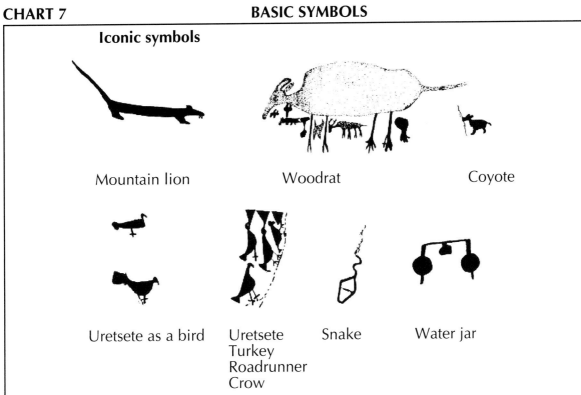

Mountain lion   Woodrat   Coyote

Uretsete as a bird   Uretsete   Snake   Water jar
                      Turkey
                      Roadrunner
                      Crow

Metaphor		Semantic Extention			
▼	Arrowhead	conflict	fight ⇌		⌛
	Terrace	cloud	altar		
	Square	land	place		
○	Circle	whole	center		
	Mound	hill	high		
	Bowl	valley	low		
	Eye	canyon			
◎	Coil	wind	snake	wave	spring
•	Dot	here			
	Barefoot	stripped for battle			

BASIC SYMBOLS

Metonymy

Tracks refering to animals that represent conditions or actions of people.

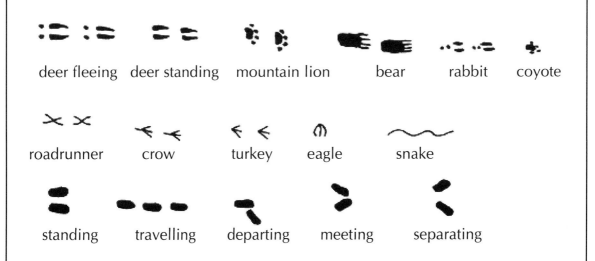

deer fleeing   deer standing   mountain lion   bear   rabbit   coyote

roadrunner   crow   turkey   eagle   snake

standing   travelling   departing   meeting   separating

Directions		Conditions	
	up		rough
	cross over		smooth
	above		many
	below		something there
	covered		nothing there
	pathway		trail

BASIC SYMBOLS

Anthropomorphic body gestures

 doing calling

barr stop

 down descend

beckon

hold own

 far (distant)

 close (nearby)

sitting

departing

stepping

kneeling

birthing

lying

talking

Zoomorphic body postures

traveling

climbing

going up

going down

dead

Sign Vehicles using anthropomorphic and zoomorphic symbol incorporations in body shape

 Turkey hands

 Square body

 Canyon shape body

 Bowl shape body

Descriptive horns

 Circle Square Dot Arrow

Backwards feet Body shape

 Breast

 Open arms Square body

 Antenna

 Rabbit ears

 Antenna

 Horns

119

GLOSSARY

Acaldes Mayores.   Senior council man.

Affinity.   The relationship in meaning or positioning that one symbol has to another symbol or symbols.

Agglutinative.   A term used to describe a word made up of several words combined into one, i.e., newspaperman.

Anasazi.   A Navajo term used in reference to prehistoric Indians who were the ancestors of the modern Pueblo.

Context.   A word, idea, or symbol that helps to clarify the meaning of a message. High and low context refers to the amount of information that is in a given communication.

Determanitive.   An additional symbol or symbols used to clarify or classify the meaning of other symbols.

El paraje de alamo.   A resting or stopping place in the trees.

Emic versus Etic.   Derived from the phonemic and phonetic linguistic analysis. Phonemics deals with the sounds and meanings of words used by a particular language and cultural group. Phonetics describes the sounds when studied by the outside observer and compared world wide. Thus emic descriptions are formulated from the "inside" cultural participant. Etic descriptions are formulated by the "outside" non-culturally participatory observer. There is a distinction now with "Ethnoscience" as emically oriented,"to discover and describe the behavioral system in its own terms..." (French 1963:398)

Goat.   An animal-like symbol not intended to represent any particular animal but rather for its use as a sign vehicle to depict lateral movement and other meanings. It is also called a quadruped.

Iariko, **Iarriko**.   Corn Mother fetish for the Keresan pueblos, made from a perfect ear of corn.

Kiva.   Pueblo ceremonial structure used for ceremonies. In some pueblos it is wholly or partially underground. It is either circular or rectangular.

La Boca. The "mouth" in Spanish, referring to the mouth of the Santa Fe Canyon.

Lexicon. A group or list of words or symbols with definitions.

Metaphor. The use of a word, phrase, or graphic motif denoting one kind of idea or object in place of another by way of suggesting a likeness or analogy between them.

Metonomy. A refference standing for something. A part that represents the whole. A sign for the thing signified.

Moiety. A dual division of the village. In most of the Rio Grande pueblos where moiety exists, an individual takes the moiety of his father, but in some pueblos if the partents   belong to different moieties their children are assigned alternately to one moiety and then another. Pueblo moieties are neither endogamous or exogamous.

Naotsete. Keresan Oral traditions tell of this mythical mother figure of all alien people particurally the Navajos.

Panel. An area of rock surface that contains petroglyphs that are related to each other. A panel may be complete in itself or relate to other panels nearby.

Patination or Patina. An oxidation process in the rock surface causing it to become darker over a long period of time.

Petroglyph. Symbols made upon a rock by pecking, incising, abrading or scratching.

Pictography. A method of communication in which pictures and ideograms are used upon any material, including rocks, a picture writing.

Quadruped. An animal-like symbol used to depict lateral action and express other meanings. It may have any number of legs or none at all. Horned quadruped have symbols added as horn-like motifs.

Rock Incorporation. A symbol purposely placed in, on or near any natural rock feature so as to incorporate the rock feature into the meaning of the message.

Semantic Extension. Additional and related meanings derived from the cultural context or suggested by the basic concept of a symbol.

Semiotics. The scientific study of symbol systems.

Sipapu (Hopi and Tewa) **Shipapu** (Keresan),   Emergence place, from inside the earth, place where Uretsete still resides.

Sign Vehicle.   A generic animal or human with symbols added on to convey more information. Body posture, exaggerated appendages, antenna, horns, ears, mixed human, animal, and insect body parts, are characteristic of the elements found in sign vehicles.

Spatial Syntax.   The meaning of a symbol is related to its proximity to other symbols in terms of directionality, reversability and simultaneity. As words of a spoken language have grammar and syntax, symbols in pictography utilize a spatial syntax.

Symbol.   A depiction or drawing used in pictography to convey any type of meaning. One of the characters, combinations, incorporations, or units of pictography.

Symbol, (basic). A symbol in its simplest form or concept that is not intended to be broken down into component parts.

Symbol Combination. Two or more basic symbols added together but each retains its basic form.

Symbol Incorporation.   Two or more basic symbols embodied in one symbol in such a way that features of both share common sections of the same symbol.

BIBLIOGRAPHY

Allen, Paula Gunn.
1986   *The Sacred Hoop.*   Boston: Beacon Press.

Bandelier, Adolf F.
1890-2   "Final Report of Investigations Among the Indians of the
                Southwestern United States, Carried on Mainly in the Years
                from 1880 -1885."   *Vol. 2 Papers of the Archaeological
                Institure of America, American series 3 and 4.*   Cambridge, Mass.

Basso, Keith H.
1972   *Semantic Aspects of Linguistic Acculturation. Culture and Cognition,
                Rules, Maps, and Plans*, ed. James Spradley, Prospect Hights: Waveland Press.

Benedict, Ruth.
1931   "Tales of the Cochiti Indians."   *Bureau of American Ethnology Bulletin 98.*
                Washington

Birenbaum,Harvey.
1988   *Myth and Mind.* Lanham,MD: University Press of America

Boas, Franz.
1928   "Keresan Text. 2 Pts." *Publication of the American Ethnological Society 8.New York*
1955   *Primitive Art*, New York: Dover Publications.

Bunzel, Ruth L.
1932   "Zuni Origin Myths." pp.545-609 in *47th Annual Report of the Bureau of
                American Ethnology for the Years 1929-30.*   Washington.

Campbell, Joseph.
1986   *The Inner Reaches of Outer Space.* New York: Harper and Row.

1949   *The Hero with a Thousand Faces*, Bollingen Series XVII, Princeton:
                Princeton University Press.

Chao, Yuen Ren.
1968   *Language and Symbolic Systems.*   Boston: Cambridge University Press.

Cirlot, J.E.
1962   *A Dictionary of Symbols.* Translated by Jack Sage. New York:
                Philosophical Library.

Clark, W.P.
1885   *The Indian Sign Language.* Reprint. Lincoln: University of Nebraska Press. 1982.

Cody, Iron Eyes.
1970   *Indian Talk, Hand Signals of the American Indians.* Happy Camp:
                Naturegraph.

Combs, Allan and Mark Holland
1990   *Synchronicity: Science, Myth and the Trickster.* New York: Paragon.

Cordell, Linda.
1984   *Prehistory of the Southwest.* School of American Research. Orlando:
                Academic Press.

Culler, Jonathan.
1981   *The Pursuit of Signs: Semiotics, Literature, Deconstruction.* Ithaca:
                Cornell University Press.
Cushing, F.
1979   *Zuni, Selected Writings of Frank Hamiltion Cushing.*
                Lincoln: University of Nebraska Press.

De George, Richard T.
1981   *Semiotic Themes.* Lawrence: University of Kansas.

Dickson, Bruce.
1979   *The Arroyo Hondo New Mexico Site Survey .* Santa Fe: University of
                New Mexico Press.

Douglas, Mary.
1982   *Natural Symbols.* New York: Pantheon.

Dumarest, Father Noel.
1919   "Notes on Cochiti, New Mexico." Elsie Clews Parsons, ed. *Memoirs of the
                American Anthropology Association* 6 (3). Lancaster, Pa.

Dutton, Burtha P.
1963   *Sun Father's Way, Kiva Murals of Kuaua, a Pueblo Ruin, Coronado State
                Monument, New Mexico.* Albuquerque: University of New Mexico Press.

Eggan, Fred.
1950   *Social Organization of the Western Pueblos.* Chicago: University of
                Chicago Press. (Reprinted 1970)

Eliade, Mircea
1974   *The Myth of the Eternal Return.* (1954) Bollingen Series XLVI: Princeton
                University Press.
1967   *Myths, Dreams and Mysteries..* (1957) New York: Harper & Row.

Ellis, Florence (Hawley)
1959   "An Outline of Laguna Pueblo History and Social Organizations."
              Southwestern Journal of Anthropology 15(4):325-347.
1976   "Where did the Pueblo People Come From?" *El Palacio* 74(3):35-43.

Espinosa, Aurelio M.
1936   "Pueblo Indian Folk Tales.." *Journal of American Folklore*, 49:69-133. Washington

Fewkes, J. Walter.
1892   "A Few Tusayan Pictographs." *American Anthropologist* 5(1):9-26.
1897   "Tusayan Totemic Signatures." *American Anthropologist* 10:1-11.
1898   "The Feather Symbol in Hopi Designs." *American Anthropologist* 11:1-14.
1904   "Ancient Pueblo and Mexican and Water Symbol." *American Anthropologist*,
              6,(4):535-538.
1906   "Hopi Ceremonial Frames." *American Anthropologist* 8 (4):664-670
1910   "The Butterfly in Hopi Myth and Ritual." *American Anthropologist*
              12(4):576-594
1973   *Designs on Prehistoric Hopi Pottery.* (1919) New York: Dover.

Firth, Ramon.
1973   *Symbols: Public and Private.* Ithaca: Cornell University Press.

Frank, Larry and Francis H. Harlow.
1974   *Historic Pottery of the Pueblo Indians 1600-1880.* Photographs by
              Bernard Lopez. Boston:New York Graphic Society.

Gauthier, Rory and David Stuart.
1984   *Prehistoric New Mexico; Background for Survey.* Albuquerque:
              University of New Mexico Press.

Geertz, Clifford
1973   *The Interpretation of Culture.* New York:Basic Books.
1983   *Local Knowledge.*New York: Basic Books.

Goldfrank, Ester S.
1927   "The Social and Ceremonial Organization of Cochiti." *Memoirs of the
              American Anthropological Association 33.* Menasha, Wis.

Goodman, Felicitas D.
1986   "Body Posture and the Religious Altered State of Consciousness: An
              Experimental Investigation." *Journal of Humanistic Psychology* 26: 81-
              118.
1988   *Ecstasy, Ritual, and Alternate Reality.* Bloomington:Indian University
              Press.
1990   *Where the Spirits Ride the Wind.* Bloomington:Indian University Press.

Gunn, John.
1917   *Schat-chen, History, Traditions, and Narratives of the Keres Indians of
              Acoma and Laguna.* Albuquerque: Albright and Anderson.

Hall, Edward T.
1976   *Beyond Culture.* New York: Anchor Books,
1983   *The Dance of Life.* New York: Anchor Books

Hackett, Charles W.,ed.
1970   *Revolt of the Pueblo Indians of New Mexico and Otermin's Attempted
                Reconquest 1680-1682.* Charmion C. Shelby, trans. 2 vols.
                Albuquerque: University of New Mexico Press.

Harrington, John Peabody and Junius Henderson.
1916   "The Ethnozoology of the Tewa Indians." *Bureau of American Ethnology
                Bulletin 56.* Washington

Hawley, Florence M.
1934   "The Significance of the Dated Prehistory of Chetro Ketl, Chaco Canyon,
                New Mexico." *Monograph Series 1(1), University of New Mexico Bulletin 246.* Albu-
                querque.
1937   "Pueblo Social Organization as a Lead to Pueblo History," *American
                Anthropologist* 39(3):504-522.

Hewett, Edgar Lee.
1938   *Pajarito Plateau and Its Ancient People.* Albuquerque: University of New
                Mexico Press.

Hibben, Frank C.
1975   *Kiva Art of the Anasazi at Pottery Mound.* Las Vegas: K.C. Publications.

Innis, Robert E.
1985   *Semiotics, an Introductory Anthology.* Bloomington: Indiana University
                Press.

Jung, Carl G.
1933   *Modern Man In Search of His Soul.* New York: Harcourt, Brace & World,
                Inc.
1956   *Symbols of Transformation* Vol. I and II. New York: Harper Torchbooks/
                Bollingen Library.
1964   *Man and His Symbols.* New York: Dell Publishing Co.
1969   *The Archetypes and the Collective Unconscious.*(1959) 2nd ed.
                Bollingen Series XX. Princeton University Press

Kessell, John L.
1979   *Kiva, Cross and Crown.* National Park Service, Department of the
                Interior, Washington D.C.

Klima, Edward S. and Ursula Bellugi,
1979   *The Signs of Language*, Cambridge: Harvard University Press.

Knaut, Andrew.
1989   *The Pueblo Revolt of 1680: Eighty Years of Cultural Tension.* Artifact, 27
                (4) 17-94. El Paso: El Paso Archaeological Society.

Lakoff, George and Mark Johnson.
1980   *Metaphors We Live By*. Chicago: University of Chicago Press.

Lakoff, George and Mark Turner.
1989   *More Than Cool Reason*. Chicago: University of Chicago Press.

Lange, Charles.
1959   *Cochiti: A New Mexico Pueblo, Past and Present*. *Austin*: University of
                Texas Press. (Reprinted: Southern Illinois University Press, Carbondale,
                1968.)

Lessa, W. and Evon Z. Vogt.
1965   *Reader in Comparative Religion; An Anthropological Approach*. New
                York: Harper and Row.

Levi-Strauss, Claude.
1955   "The Structural Study of Myth." *Myth, a Symposium*, Sebeok ed.
                Bloomington: University of Indiana Press.
1963a   *Structural Anthropology*. Translated by Claire Jacobson and Brooke G.
                Schoepf. New York: Basic Books.
1963b   *Totemism*.   Boston: Beacon Press.
1966   *The Savage Mind*. Chicago: University of Chicago Press.
1982   *The Way of the Masks*. Translated by Sylvia Modelski. Seattle: University
                of Washington Press.
1985   *The View from Afar*. New York: Basic Books.
1988   *The Jealous Potter*. Chicago: University of Chicago Press.

Mallery, Garrick.
1893   "Picture Writing of the American Indians." *Tenth Annual Report of the
                Bureau of Ethnology*, 1888-89, (reprint,1972) New York: Dover.

Maranda, P.
1972   *Mythology, Selected Readings*.. England: Penguin Education Books.

Martineau, L.
1973   *The Rocks Begin to Speak*, Las Vegas: K.C.   Publications.

Martineau, La Van, B.K. Swartz and Charles Houch.
1981   "The Use of Indian Gesture Language for the Interpretation of North
                American Petroglyphs: A Trial Analysis." *The Occasional Papers of the
                American Committee To Advance the Study of Petroglyphs and
                Pictographs*, Vol. 1 Indiana University.

Martineau, La Van and Alex Shephard.
1985   *Clear Creek Project*, Paiute Indian Tribe of Utah,

Martineau, L.
1988, 1989   Personal Communication.

Matejka, Ladislav and Irwin R. Titunik.
1976   *Semiotics of Art*. Cambridge: MIT press

Miller, Jay.
1980   "The Matter of the (Thoughtful) Heart: Centrality, Focality, or Overlap."
            Journal of Anthropological Research: 338-342
1989   "Deified Mind Among the Keresan Pueblos." pp. 151-156 in *General
            and Amerindian Ethnolinguistics. In Remembrance of Stanley Newman.*
            Edited by Mary Ritchie Key and Henry M. Hoeningswald . Berlin:
            Mouton de Gruyter.

Olsen, N.
1985   "Hovenweep Rock Art: an Anasazi Visual Communication System."
            Occasional Paper 14, Institute of Archaeology. Los Angeles: University
            of California Press.
1989   "Social Roles of Animal Iconography: Implications for Archaeology from
            Hopi and Zuni Ethnographic Sources." *Animals Into Art,* H. Morphy,ed.
            London:Unwin Hyman.

Ortiz, A.
1972   *New Perspectives on the Pueblos.* Albuquerque: University of New
            Mexico Press.
1989   *The Tribal World as a Mosaic.* Lecture for the Santa Fe Trails Association
            Conference, Santa Fe.

Parsons, Elsie Clews.
1926   "Tewa Tales. Memoirs of the American Folk-Lore Society",19. New York.
1932   Isleta, New Mexico. *47th Annual Report of the Bureau of American
            Ethnology.* Washington:D.C.
1931   "Laguna Tales." *Journal of American Folklore,* 44:137-142. Washington: D.C.
1938   "The Humpback Flute Player of the Southwest", *American Anthropologist,*
            No. 40:337-338.
1939   *Pueblo Religion, Vol. 1 and 2,* Chicago: University of Chicago Press.

Patterson, Carol (Patterson-Rudolph).
1987   "Uretsete and Naotsete Genesis Myth from Cochiti Pueblo." *Artifact*
            Vol. 26 (1):1-23 El Paso: El Paso Archaeological Society.
1989   *Sign Language and Petroglyphs. Exploring Rock Art.* Donald Cyr, ed.
            Santa Barbara: Stonehenge Viewpoint.
1990   Water Jar Boy. American Indian Culture and Research Journal. vol (14)
            Los Angles: UCLA Press.

Peng, F. C.
1981   "Sign Language and Language Acquistion in Man and Ape." *AAAS
            Selected Symposium.* West View Press

Purley, Anthony
1974   "Keres Pueblo Concepts of Deity." *American Indian Culture and Research Journal.*
            1 (1) 29-32 LA:UCLA

Rohn, Arthur.
1989   *Rock Art of Bandelier National Monument.* Albuquerque: University of
            New Mexico Press.

Schaafsma, Polly.
1980   *Indian Rock Art of the Southwest.* Albuquerque: University of New Mexico Press.
1989   Supper or Symbol: Roadrunner Tracks in Southwest Art and Ritual,
                    Animals Into Art, Howard Morphy, ed. London:Unwin Hyman.

Scheoder, Albert.
1972   "Rio Grande Ethnohistory", Pp. 41-70 *New Perspectives on the Pueblos.*
                    Alfonso Ortiz,ed. Albuquerque: University of New Mexico Press.
1979   "Pueblos Abandoned in Historic Times." *Southwest, Handbook of North*
                    American Indians. vol.9. Washington: Smithsonian Institution.

Schoolcraft, Henry R.
1851-1857   *Historical and Statistical Information Respecting the History, Condition*
                    and Prospects of the Indian Tribes of the United States. 6 vol.
                    Philadelphia: Lippincott, Grambo.

Seattle, Chief
1854   "Chief Seattle's Speech of 1854 to Seattle Washington Territory." *Seattle*
                    Sunday Star, Washington Territory, October 26, 1887.

Sebeok, Thomas A.
1981   *The Play of Musement.* Bloomington:Indiana University Press.
1987   *Sight, Sound and Sense.* Bloomington: Indiana University Press.
1955   *Myth, a Symposium.* Bloomington: Indiana University Press.

Sebeok, Thomas and Jean Umiker.
1987   *Monastic Sign Languages.* New York: Mouton De Gruyter.
1978   *Aboriginal Sign Languages of the Americas and Australia* Vol 1 and 2.
                    New York: Plenum Press.

Sebeok, Jean Umiker and Irene Portis Winner,
1979   *Semiotics of Culture.* The Hague: Mouton.

Skelly, Madge.
1979   *Amer-Indian Gesture Code Based on Universal American Indian Hand*
                    Talk. New York: Elsevier Science Publishing.

Spradley, James P.
1972   *Culture and Cognition, Rules, Maps and Plans.* Prospect Heights:
                    Waveland Press.

Stevenson, Matildia Cox.
1984   "The Sia." *Eleventh Annual Report of the Bureau of American Ethnology*
                    1889-90. Washington.

Stirling, M.
1942   "The Origin Myth of Acoma." *Bureau of American Ethnology Bulletin 135.*
                    Washington.

Stokoe, W. C. Jr.
1972   *Semiotics and Human Sign Languages.* The Hague: Mouton.

Tomkins, W.
1930   *Universal American Indian Sign Language.* San Diego.

Tyler, H. A.
1979   *Pueblo Birds and Myths.* Tulsa: University of Oklahoma Press.
1975   *Pueblo Animals and Myths.* University of Oklahoma Press
1964   *Pueblo Gods and Myths.* University of Oklahoma Press

Voth, Henry R.
1905   *Traditions of the Hopi.* Field Museum of Natural History Publication 96,
                Anthropological Series 8. Chicago

Victoria Neufeldt and David B. ed.
1988   *Websters New World Dictionary of American English*, New York: Simon and
                Schuster, Inc.

White, Leslie A.
1932   "The Acoma Indians." *47th Annual Report of the Bureau of American
                Ethnology,* 1929-30, Washington
1932   "The Pueblo of San Felipe." *Memoirs of the American Anthropological
                Association* 38. Menasha, Wis.
1935   "The Pueblo of Santo Domingo," *Memoirs of the American
                Anthropological Association* 43. Menasha Wis.
1962   "The Pueblo of Sia, New Mexico," *Bureau of American Ethnology Bulletin*
                184. Washington.

Wood, Nancy.
1974   *Many Winters.*   New York: Doubleday.

Young, Jane.
1985   "Images of Power and Power of Images." *Journal of American Folklore*, Vol. 98:3-48.
1988   *Signs From the Ancestors.* Albuquerque: University of New Mexico
                Press.